JOHANNES ITTEN

THE ART OF COLOR

The subjective experience and objective rationale of color

Translated by Ernst van Haagen

 VAN NOSTRAND REINHOLD COMPANY
NEW YORK · CINCINNATI · TORONTO · LONDON · MELBOURNE

Jan 1974

Van Nostrand Reinhold Company,
Regional Offices:
New York, Cincinnati, Chicago, Millbrae, Dallas

Van Nostrand Reinhold Company International Offices:
London, Toronto, Melbourne

Copyright © 1961 and 1973 by Otto Maier Verlag Ravensburg
Originally published in Germany under the title "Kunst der
Farbe"
Library of Congress Catalog Card Number 61-11190
ISBN 0-442-24037-6

Printed in Germany
Color separation: Seiler & Jehle, Augsburg
Composition: Buch- und Verlagsdruckerei Göppel, Ravensburg
Printing: J. Fink, Kemnat near Stuttgart

Published in the United States of America
by Van Nostrand Reinhold Company
A Division of Litton Educational Publishing, Inc.
450 West 33rd Street, New York, N. Y. 10001

16 15 14 13 12 11 10 9 8 7 6

CONTENTS

LIST OF PLATES

INTRODUCTION

Learning from books and teachers is like traveling by carriage, so we are told in the Veda. The thought goes on, "But the carriage will serve only while one is on the highroad. He who reaches the end of the highroad will leave the carriage and walk afoot."

In this book I shall try to build a serviceable conveyance that will help all who are interested in the problems of color artistry. One may travel carriageless and by unblazed trails, but progress is then slow and the journey perilous. If a high and distant goal is to be attained, then it is advisable to take a carriage at first in order to advance swiftly and safely.

Many of my students have helped me to find materials with which to build, and I am deeply indebted to them. The doctrine to be developed here is an aesthetic color theory originating in the experience and intuition of a painter. For the artist, effects are decisive, rather than agents as studied by physics and chemistry. Because color effects are in the eye of the beholder, the many color plates were indispensable. Yet the deepest and truest secrets of color effect are, I know, invisible even to the eye, and are beheld by the heart alone. The essential eludes conceptual formulation.

In the realm of aesthetics, are there general rules and laws of color for the artist, or is the aesthetic appreciation of colors governed solely by subjective opinion? Students often ask this question, and my answer is always the same: "If you, unknowing, are able to create masterpieces in color, then un-knowledge is your way. But if you are unable to create masterpieces in color out of your un-knowledge, then you ought to look for knowledge."

Doctrines and theories are best for weaker moments. In moments of strength, problems are solved intuitively, as if of themselves.

Close study of the great master colorists has firmly convinced me that all of them possessed a science of color. For me, the theories of Goethe, Runge, Bezold, Chevreul and Hölzel have been invaluable.

I hope to be able to resolve a great many color problems in this book. We are not merely to expound objective principles and rules, but also to explore and survey the subjective predicament, as it pertains to critical taste in the realm of color.

We can be released from subjective bondage only through knowledge and awareness of objective principles.

In music, the theory of composition has long been an important and accepted part of a professional education. However, a musician may know counterpoint and still be a dull composer, if he lacks insight and inspiration. Just so, a painter may know all the resources of composition in form and color, yet remain sterile if inspiration be denied him.

It has been said that genius is 99 per cent perspiration and 1 per cent inspiration. There was a debate in the press years ago between Richard Strauss and Hans Pfitzner about the relative shares of inspiration and contrapuntal deduction in the process of composition. Strauss wrote that four to six bars were inspiration in his own works, and the rest elaboration. Pfitzner replied, "It may well be that Strauss is inspired only through four to six bars, but I have noticed that Mozart often composes many pages together under inspiration."

Leonardo, Dürer, Grünewald, El Greco and the rest did not scorn to examine their artistic media intellectually. How could the Isenheim altarpiece have been produced, had not its creator pondered form and color?

Knowledge of the laws of design need not imprison, it can liberate from indecision and vacillating perception. What we call laws of color, obviously, can be no more than fragmentary, given the complexity and irrationality of color effects.

In the course of time, the human mind has penetrated many mysteries in their essence or in their mechanism — the rainbow, thunder and lightning, gravity and so on. But they are still mysteries for all that.

Delacroix wrote, "The elements of color theory have been neither analyzed nor taught in our schools of art, because in France it is considered superfluous to study the laws of color, according to the saying 'Draftsmen may be made, but colorists are born.' Secrets of color theory? Why call those principles secrets which all artists must know and all should have been taught?" (Les Artistes de mon Temps).

As the tortoise draws its limbs into its shell at need, so the artist reserves his scientific principles when working intuitively. But would it be better for the tortoise to have no legs?

Color is life; for a world without colors appears to us as dead. Colors are primordial ideas, children of the aboriginal colorless light and its counterpart, colorless darkness. As flame begets light, so light engenders colors. Colors are the children of light, and light is their mother. Light, that first phenomenon of the world, reveals to us the spirit and living soul of the world through colors.

Nothing affects the human mind more dramatically than the apparition of a gigantic color corona in the heavens. Thunder and lightning frighten us; but the colors of the rainbow and the northern lights soothe and elevate the soul. The rainbow is accounted a symbol of peace.

The word and its sound, form and its color, are vessels of a transcendental essence that we dimly surmise. As sound lends sparkling color to the spoken word, so color lends psychically resolved tone to form.

The primeval essence of color is a phantasmagorical resonance, light become music. At the moment when thought, concept, formulation, touch upon color, its spell is broken, and we hold in our hands a corpse.

In the tinted monuments of past ages, we can trace the emotional dispositions of vanished peoples. The ancient Egyptians and Greeks greatly delighted in varicolored design.

The Chinese were accomplished painters from early times. An emperor of the Han dynasty is recorded in 80 B.C. to have kept storehouses — a museum — of paintings collected by him, said to have been of great and colorful beauty. In the T'ang period (618 - 907 A.D.), there arose a strongly colored mural and panel painting. About the same time, new yellow, red, green and blue ceramic glazes were developed. In the Sung dynasty (960 - 1279 A.D.), the sense of color was extraordinarily cultivated. Pictorial colors became more varied and at once more naturalistic. Ceramics evolved many new glazes of matchless beauty, such as celadon and clair de lune.

Strongly colored Roman and Byzantine polychrome mosaics from the first millennium of the Christian era have been preserved in Europe. Mosaic art placed high demands on coloristic powers, because each color area is composed of numerous point elements, each requiring consideration and choice. The mosaic artists of Ravenna in the fifth and sixth centuries were able to produce many different effects with complementary colors.

The mausoleum of Galla Placidia is dominated by a remarkable colored atmosphere of gray light. This effect is produced by bathing the blue mosaic walls of the interior in an orange light, filtered through narrow windows of orange-tinted alabaster. Orange and blue are complementary colors, the mixing of which yields gray. As the visitor moves about the shrine, he receives different quantities of light which is alternately accented blue and orange, the walls reflecting these colors at ever-changing angles. This interplay gives an impression of suffusion with color.

In the early medieval illuminations of the Irish monks in the eighth and ninth centuries, we find a palette of great variety and subtlety. Most astonishing in their radiant power are those pages where the many different colors are rendered in equal brilliance. The resulting vivid cold-warm effects are such as we do not find again until the Impressionists and Van Gogh. Some leaves of the Book of Kells, for logic of chromatic execution and organic rhythm of line, are as magnificent and pure as a Bach fugue. The sensitivity and artistic intelligence of these "abstract" miniaturists had their monumental counterpart in the stained glass of the Middle Ages. Early stained glass employed only a few different colors, and therefore seems crude, for glassmaking techniques afforded few colors as yet. Anyone who has spent a day studying the windows in the cathedral at Chartres in the changing light, and has seen the setting sun kindle the great rose window to a splendid culminating chord, will never forget the supernal beauty of that moment.

The Romanesque and Early Gothic artists, in their mural and tablet paintings, used colors as symbolic expressions. Therefore they endeavored to produce unequivocal, unclouded tones. Simple and clear symbolic effect was sought, rather than multitudinous shadings and chromatic variations. Form received a similar treatment.

Giotto and the Sienese school may have been the first painters to indivualize the human figure in form and color, thus initiating a development that was to lead to the imposing throng of artist personalities encountered in the Europe of the fifteenth, sixteenth and seventeenth centuries.

In the first half of the fifteenth century, the brothers Hubert and Jan van Eyck began to construct patterns of composition around the local colors of the person or thing represented. These local colors, through dull and bright, light and dark tones, produced realistic images very closely approaching nature. Color became a means of characterizing natural objects. The Ghent altarpiece was finished in 1432, and in 1434 Jan van Eyck executed the first Gothic portrait, the double portrait of Arnolfini and his lady.

Francesca (1410 - 1492) painted individuals in sharp outline and clearly expressive areas, with balancing complementary colors. The hues are rare tones especially characteristic of the artist.

Leonardo (1452 - 1519) rejected strong coloration. He painted in infinitesimal tonal gradations, organized in the case of his "Virgin of the Grotto" into two principal planes. "St. Jerome" and the "Adoration" are composed entirely in sepia tones of light and shade.

Titian (1477 - 1576) in his early work set homogeneous color areas against each other in isolation. Later, he progressively resolved such areas into cool and warm, light and dark, dull and intense modulations, perhaps best exemplified by the "Bella", in the Pitti galleries. In the works of his old age, he evolved objects out of one principal hue and many variant tints and shades. The "Ecce Homo" is an example.

El Greco (1545 - 1614) was a pupil of Titian. He brought his master's polytonality back to large, expressive color areas. His strange, frequently shocking color renditions cease to represent local colors, but are abstract, matching the psychically expressive requirements of the theme. This is why El Greco is considered a progenitor of nonobjective painting. His color areas do not denote objective categories. They have been organized into sheer pictorial polyphony.

Grünewald (1475 - 1528), a century earlier, had solved this same problem. Where El Greco's shades are always sharply and characteristically defined by gray and black tones, Grünewald set color against color. Through what may be called an objective mastery of the universe of color, he discovered the appropriate colors for each pictorial motif. The Isenheim altarpiece in all its parts shows such multiplicity of color quality, effect and expression as to be properly called an intellectually universal color composition. The Annunciation, Angel Choir (Plate IX), Crucifixion, Resurrection (Plate XXVII), are pictures utterly different from each other, in form as well as color.

In fact, Grünewald sacrificed decorative unity of the altarpiece as a whole to artistic truth of the individual theme. He set himself above the scholastic canon, in order to be truthful and objective. However, the psychologically expressive power of his colors, their symbolic verity, and their realistic signification — all these three potentialities of color are, in a deeper sense, fused into unity.

Rembrandt (1606 - 1669) is considered the exemplar of chiaroscuro painters. Though Leonardo, Titian and El Greco used chiaroscuro as a means of expression, Rembrandt's work is altogether different. He felt color as a dense material. With gray and blue or yellow and red transparent tones, he created an effect of depth that has a remarkably transfigured life of its own. Employing a mixed paste of tempera and oil paints, he achieved textures radiating an uncommonly affecting realism (Plate VI, Man in Golden Helmet). In Rembrandt, color becomes materialized light-energy, charged with tension. Pure colors often shine like jewels in dull settings.

El Greco and Rembrandt carry us into the problems of baroque color. In the more extreme baroque architectures, static space is resolved into space with dynamic rhythm. Color is enlisted in the same service. It is detached from its objective denotation and becomes an abstract means of rhythmic articulation. Ultimately, it is used to assist depth illusions. The work of the Viennese painter Maulbertsch (1724 - 1796) exhibits such characteristically baroque coloration.

In the art of the Empire and Classical periods, coloration is confined to black, white, gray, sparingly enlivened with some few chromatic colors. This style, giving an effect of realism and sobriety, was supplanted by Romanticism. The beginning of the Romantic movement in painting is identified with Turner (1775 - 1851) and Constable (1776 - 1837) in England. Its greatest exponents in Germany were Caspar David Friedrich (1774 - 1840) and Philipp Otto Runge (1777 - 1810). These painters employed color as a psychico-expressive medium, to lend "mood" to landscape. Constable, for example, would not apply homogeneous green to canvas, but would resolve it into minute gradations of light and dark, cold and warm, dull and vivid tones. Color areas were thus rendered subtly vital. Turner produced some non-objective color compositions that would warrant listing him as the first "abstractionist" among European painters.

Delacroix (1798 - 1863) saw Turner's and Constable's work when he was in London. Their colorism interested him deeply, and on his return, he re-did some paintings of his own in the same spirit, thereby causing a sensation at the 1820 Salon de Paris. Delacroix was actively concerned with color problems and principles throughout his lifetime.

General interest in the influence and rationale of color prevailed early in the nineteenth century. Runge published his color theory using the sphere as a coordinate system in 1810. Goethe's major work on color appeared likewise in 1810, and in 1816 Schopenhauer published his treatise "On Vision and Colors." The chemist M. E. Chevreul (1786 - 1889), manager of the Gobelin works in Paris, published his "De la Loi du Contraste Simultané des Couleurs et de l'Assortiment des Objets Coloris" in 1839. This work was to become the scientific foundation of Impressionist and Neo-Impressionist painting.

Intensive study of nature led the Impressionists to an entirely new color rendition. Study of sunlight, which alters the local tones of natural objects, and study of light in the atmospheric world of landscape, provided the Impressionist painters with new essential patterns. Monet explored these phenomena conscientiously, requiring a fresh canvas to represent a landscape at each hour of the day, so that the progress of the sun and resulting change in color of the light and reflections might be truly rendered. The best demonstration of this procedure are his cathedral paintings, on display in the Jeu de Paume Museum in Paris.

The Neo-Impressionists divided color areas into point elements. They affirmed that mixing pigments breaks the power of the colors. The dots of pure color were to become mingled only in the eye of the viewer.

The color theories of Chevreul were of signal aid to the Impressionists.

Proceeding from Impressionist ideas, Cézanne arrived at a logically developed color construction. It was his task to fashion Impressionism into something "substantial"; his pictures were to stand upon formal and chromatic principle. Apart from his rhythmic and formal contributions, in color he rejected the Pointillist technique of division, returning to continuous areas modulated internally. To him, modulating a color meant varying it between cold and warm, light and dark, or dull and intense. Such modulation throughout the picture area accomplished new, vivid harmonies.

Titian and Rembrandt had contented themselves with color modulations of faces and figures; Cézanne was now integrating the whole picture formally, rhythmically and chromatically. In the still life "Apples and Oranges" (Plate XII), this new integration is clearly apparent. Cézanne wished to remold nature at a higher level. To do this, he employed the cold-warm contrast with musical, ethereal effect. Cézanne, and Bonnard after him, composed some pictures entirely on the cold-warm theme.

Matisse refrained from modulation, to again express simple, luminous areas in subjective equilibrium. With Braque, Derain and Vlaminck, he belonged to the Paris group Les Fauves.

The Cubists – Picasso, Braque and Gris – used colors for their light-dark values. They were primarily interested in form. They analyzed the shapes of objects into abstract geometric forms, obtaining relief-like effects by tonal gradation.

The Expressionists – Munch, Kirchner, Heckel, Nolde, and the Blauer Reiter painters Kandinsky, Marc, Macke, Klee – were attempting to restore psychological content to painting. Their creative aim was to represent internalized and spiritualized experience by means of shapes and colors.

Kandinsky began painting non-objective pictures about 1908. He contended that every color has its proper expressional value, and that it is therefore possible to create meaningful realities without representing objects.

Adolf Hölzel became the center of a group of young painters in Stuttgart who attended his lectures on color theory, based on the discoveries of Goethe, Schopenhauer and Bezold.

Between 1912 and 1917, in various parts of Europe independently, artists were at work producing what may be subsumed under the collective name "art concret". Among them were Kupka, Delaunay, Malewitsch, Itten, Arp, Mondrian and Vantongerloo. Their paintings represent non-objective, usually geometric forms and pure spectral colors in the guise of actual corporeal objects. The intellectually apperceptible forms and colors are media that admit of clear pictorial arrangement.

More recently, Mondrian made a further contribution. He used pure yellow, red, and blue, like weights, to construct paintings whose form and color coincide in the effect of static equilibrium. He aimed not at surreptitious expression, nor at intellectual symbolism, but at real, optically distinct, concrete harmonic patterns (Plate IV).

The Surrealists – Max Ernst, Salvador Dali and the others – have employed colors as means of expression for the pictorial realization of their "irrealities."

As for the Tachistes, they are "anomalists" in color as well as in form.

Developments in color chemistry, fashion, and color photography have aroused a broad general interest in colors, and the color sensitivity of the individual has been greatly refined. But this contemporary interest in color is almost wholly visual, material in character, and not grounded in intellectual and emotional experience. It is a superficial, external toying with metaphysical forces.

Colors are forces, radiant energies that affect us positively or negatively, whether we are aware of it or not. The artists in stained glass used color to create a supramundane, mystical atmosphere which would transport the meditations of the worshiper to a spiritual plane. The effects of colors should be experienced and understood, not only visually, but also psychologically and symbolically.

The problems of color can thus be examined from several aspects.

The physicist studies the nature of the electromagnetic energy vibrations and particles involved in the phenomena of light, the several origins of color phenomena such as the prismatic dispersion of white light, and the problems of pigmentation. He investigates mixtures of chromatic light, spectra of the elements, frequencies and wave lengths of colored light rays. Measurement and classification of colors are also topics of physical research.

The chemist studies the molecular structure of dyes and pigments, problems of color fastness, vehicles, and preparation of synthetic dyes. Color chemistry today embraces an extraordinarily wide field of industrial research and production.

The physiologist investigates the various effects of light and colors on our visual apparatus – eye and brain – and their anatomical relationships and functions. Research on light- and dark-adapted vision and on chromatic color vision occupies an important place. The phenomenon of afterimages is another physiological topic.

The psychologist is interested in problems of the influence of color radiation on our mind and spirit. Color symbolism, and the subjective perception and discrimination of colors, are important psychological problems. Expressive color effects – what Goethe called the ethico-aesthetic values of colors – likewise fall within the psychologist's province.

The artist, finally, is interested in color effects from their aesthetic aspect, and needs both physiological and psychological information.

Discovery of relationships, mediated by the eye and brain, between color agents and color effects in man, is a major concern of the artist. Visual, mental and spiritual phenomena are multiply interrelated in the realm of color and the color arts.

Contrast effects and their classification are a proper starting point in the study of color aesthetics. The problems of subjectively conditioned color perception are especially pertinent to art education and scholarship, architecture and commercial design.

Color aesthetics may be approached from these three directions:

Impression (visually)

Expression (emotionally)

Construction (symbolically)

It is interesting to notice that in pre-Columbian Peru, the use of color is symbolic in the Tiahuanaco culture, expressional in the Paracas, and impressional in the Chimu.

Among historical peoples, there have been styles using colors as symbolic values only, either to identify social strata or castes, or as symbolic terms for mythological or religious ideas.

In China, yellow, the most luminous color, was reserved to the emperor, the Son of Heaven. None other might wear a yellow garment; yellow was a symbol of supreme wisdom and enlightenment. Again, when the Chinese wear white on occasions of mourning, this signifies an escorting of the departed into the kingdom of purity and of heaven. The white color is not an expression of personal grief; it is worn by way of assisting the dead to a state of perfection.

When a pre-Columbian painter in Mexico put a red-clad figure into his composition, it was understood to pertain to the earth god Xipe-totec and therefore to the eastern sky, with its signification of sunrise, birth, youth and springtime. In other words, the figure was colored red not from considerations of visual aesthetics or to convey emotional expression; its color was symbolic, like a logogram or hieroglyph.

The Roman Catholic hierarchy has its distinguishing symbolic colors, including the cardinal crimson and the papal white. In the observance of ecclesiastical feasts, vestments of prescribed colors are worn. Inevitably, sound religious art makes symbolic use of color.

When it comes to studying the emotionally expressive power of colors, our great masters are El Greco and Grünewald.

The visually impressive component of coloration was taken as the cornerstone of their pictorial work by Velásquez and Zurbarán, by Van Eyck and the still-life and interior painters of the Low Countries, by the Le Nain brothers, and later by Chardin, Ingres, Courbet, Leibl and others. Leibl, particularly painstaking, narrowly observed the minutest modulations of colors in nature, and painted them as minutely on his canvases. He never worked on a picture unless he had the natural model before him. The painters commonly referred to as Impressionists, such as Manet, Monet, Degas, Pissarro, Renoir and Sisley, studying the local colors of objects as modified by changing sunlight, at last increasingly neglected local colors and addressed their attention to the color vibrations produced by light on surfaces and in the atmosphere at different times of day. (See Plate XI, Monet, Houses of Parliament.)

Only those who love color are admitted to its beauty and immanent presence. It affords utility to all, but unveils its deeper mysteries only to its devotees.

Having spoken of three different points of view for purposes of studying color – constructional, expressional and impressional – I would not omit to say this: Symbolism without visual accuracy and without emotional force would be mere anemic formalism; visually impressive effect without symbolic verity and emotional power would be banal imitative naturalism; emotional effect without constructive symbolic content or visual strength would be limited to the plane of sentimental expression. Of course every artist will work according to his temperament, and must emphasize one or another of these aspects.

To avoid confusion, I should like to define two terms.

By the quality of a color, I mean its position or location inside the color circle or solid. Both the pure unclouded colors and all their possible mixtures with each other yield unique chromas. The color green, for example, may be mixed with yellow, orange, red, violet, blue, white or black, and acquires a specific unique quality by each of these admixtures. Each possible modification of a color effect by simultaneous influences likewise generates specific color qualities.

When we are to specify the degree of lightness or darkness of a color, we may speak of its quantity or brilliance. This is what I occasionally refer to as tonal gradation. Brilliance can be varied in two ways; firstly, by mixing a color with white, black or gray, and secondly by mixing it with another color of unlike brilliance.

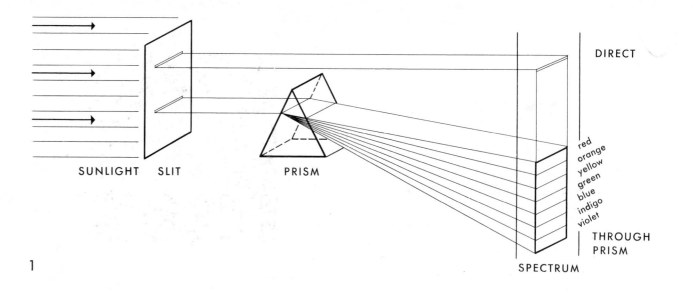

SUNLIGHT   SLIT   PRISM   DIRECT

red
orange
yellow
green
blue
indigo
violet

THROUGH PRISM

SPECTRUM

1

COLOR PHYSICS

In 1676, Sir Isaac Newton, using a triangular prism, analyzed white sunlight into a spectrum of colors. Such a spectrum contains all hues except purple.

Newton performed his experiment as follows (Fig. 1): Sunlight entering through a slit falls upon the prism. In the prism, the ray of white light is dispersed into the spectral colors. The dispersed ray of light can be projected on a screen to display the spectrum. A continuous band of color ranges from red through orange, yellow, green, blue, to violet. If this image is collected by means of a converging lens, addition of the colors will yield white light once again.

These colors are produced by refraction. There are other physical ways of generating colors, such as interference, diffraction, polarization and fluorescence.

If we divide the spectrum into two parts, for example red-orange-yellow and green-blue-violet, and collect each of these two groups with a converging lens, the result will be two mixed colors, whose mixture with each other in turn yields white.

Two kinds of colored light whose mixture with each other yields white are called complementary.

If we isolate one hue from the prismatic spectrum, for example green, and collect the remaining colors – red, orange, yellow, blue, violet – with a lens, the mixed color obtained will be red, i.e. the complementary color of the green we

isolated. If we take out yellow, the remaining colors – red, orange, green, blue, violet – will yield violet, the complementary of yellow.

Each spectral hue is the complement of the mixture of all the other spectral hues.

We cannot see the component hues in a mixed color. The eye is not like the musical ear, which can single out any of the individual tones in a mixture.

Colors result from light waves, a particular kind of electromagnetic energy. The human eye can perceive light of wave lengths between 400 and 700 millimicrons only.
1 micron or $1\,\mu$ = $^1/_{1000}$ mm. = $^1/_{1000000}$ m.
1 millimicron or $1\,m\mu$ = $^1/_{1000000}$ mm.

The wave lengths and corresponding frequencies, in cycles per second, for each prismatic color, are as follows:

Color	Wave Length, mμ	Frequency, cps
Red	800 - 650	400 - 470 million million
Orange	640 - 590	470 - 520 million million
Yellow	580 - 550	520 - 590 million million
Green	530 - 490	590 - 650 million million
Blue	480 - 460	650 - 700 million million
Indigo	450 - 440	700 - 760 million million
Violet	430 - 390	760 - 800 million million

The harmonic interval from red to violet is approximately the double; i.e. an octave.

Each hue can be accurately defined by specifying its wave length or frequency. The light waves are not in themselves colored. Color arises in the human eye and brain. How we discriminate these wave lengths is not yet well understood. We know

only that the several colors arise from qualitative differences in photosensitivity.

It remains to consider the important question of the colors of objects. If we hold a red and a green color filter, for example, in front of an arc lamp, the two together will give black, or darkness. The red filter absorbs all the rays in the spectrum except for the red interval, and the green filter absorbs all but the green. So no color is left over, and the effect is black. Colors resulting from absorption are known as subtractive colors.

The colors of objects are chiefly subtractive colors of this nature. A red vessel looks red because it absorbs all other colors of light, and reflects only red.

When we say, "This bowl is red," what we are really saying is that the molecular constitution of its surface is such as to absorb all light rays but those of red. The bowl does not have color in itself; light generates the color.

If red paper – a surface absorbing all rays but the red – is illuminated with green light, the paper will appear black, because the green light contains no red to be reflected.

All the painter's colors are pigmentary, or corporeal. They are absorptive colors, and their mixtures are governed by the rules of subtraction. When complementary colors, or combinations containing the three primaries, yellow, red, and blue, are mixed in certain proportions, the subtractive resultant is black.

The analogous mixture of prismatic, non-corporeal colors yields white as an additive resultant.

The color agent is the physically or chemically definable and analyzable pigment, the colorant. It acquires human meaning and content by optic and cerebral perception.

The eye and the mind achieve distinct perception through comparison and contrast. The value of a chromatic color may be determined by relation to an achromatic color – black, white, gray – or to one or more other chromatic colors. Color perception is the psychophysiological reality as distinguished from the physicochemical reality of color.

Psychophysiological color reality is what I call color effect. Color agent and color effect coincide only in the case of harmonious polytones. In all other cases, the agency of color is simultaneously transmuted into a new effect. Some examples will demonstrate this.

We know that a white square on a black ground will look larger than a black square of the same size on a white ground. The white reaches out and overflows the boundary, whereas the black contracts.

A light-gray square looks dark on a white background; the same light-gray square looks light on a black ground.

Fig. 2: A yellow square on white and on black. On white, yellow looks darker, with an effect of fine, delicate warmth. On black, yellow acquires extreme brilliance and a cold, aggressive quality of expression.

Fig. 3: A red square on white and on black. Red looks very dark on white, and its brilliance scarcely asserts itself. On black, however, red radiates luminous warmth.

Fig. 4: A blue square on white and on black. On white, the effect of blue is one of darkness and depth. The surrounding white square looks brighter than in the case of yellow. On black, the blue takes on a brilliant character, with deep luminescence of hue.

5

Fig. 5: A gray square on ice blue and on red-orange. The gray on ice blue looks reddish, while the same gray on red-orange looks bluish. The difference is very plain when the two configurations are viewed simultaneously.

When agent and effect do not coincide, we have a discordant, dynamic, unreal and fugitive expression. It is this power of material and chromatic realities to generate unreal vibrations that affords the artist his opportunity to express the ineffable.

The phenomena instanced by these experiments might well be grouped under the head of "simultaneity." The possibility of simultaneous mutation suggests the advisability, in the process of color composition, of beginning with color effect, and developing the size and shape of areas accordingly.

Once a theme has been conceived, the design must follow that primary and ruling conception. If color is the chief vehicle of expression, composition must begin with color areas, and these will determine the lines. He who first draws lines and then adds color will never succeed in producing a clear, intense color effect. Colors have dimensions and directionality of their own, and delineate areas in their own way.

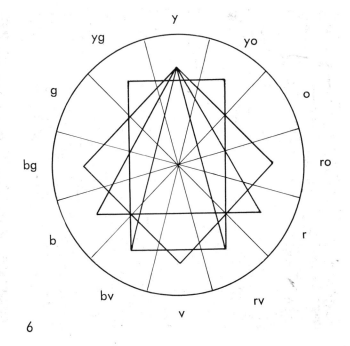

6

CONCORD OF COLORS

When people speak of color harmony, they are evaluating the joint effect of two or more colors. Experience and experiments with subjective color combinations show that individuals differ in their judgments of harmony and discord.

The color combinations called "harmonious" in common speech usually are composed of closely similar chromas, or else of different colors in the same shades. They are combinations of colors that meet without sharp contrast. As a rule, the assertion of harmony or discord simply refers to an agreeable-disagreeable or attractive-unattractive scale. Such judgments are personal sentiments without objective force. The concept of color harmony should be removed from the realm of subjective attitude into that of objective principle.

Harmony implies balance, symmetry of forces.

An examination of physiological phenomena in color vision will bring us closer to a solution of the problem.

If we gaze for some time at a green square and then close our eyes, we see, as an afterimage, a red square. If we look at a red square, the afterimage is a green square. This experiment may be repeated with any color, and the afterimage always turns out to be of the complementary color. The eye posits the complementary color; it seeks to restore equilibrium of itself. This phenomenon is referred to as successive contrast.

In another experiment, we insert a gray square in an area of pure color of the same brilliance. On green, the gray will look reddish gray. On red, it will seem greenish gray; on violet, yellowish gray; and on yellow, violet-gray. Each color causes the gray to be tinged with its complementary. Pure colors also have the tendency to shift other chromatic colors towards their own complement. This phenomenon is referred to as simultaneous contrast.

Successive and simultaneous contrast suggest that the human eye is satisfied, or in equilibrium, only when the complemental relation is established. Let us approach this idea from a different direction.

In 1797, in Nicholson's Journal, Rumford published his hypothesis that colors are harmonious if they mix to give white. As a physicist, he was speaking in terms of colored light. In the section on color physics, we stated that if one color of a spectrum, say red, is suppressed, and the other colored light rays — yellow, orange, violet, blue and green — are collected with a lens, the sum of these residual colors will be green, or the complementary of the color suppressed. Physical mixture of a color with its complementary color yields the sum total of the colors, or white; pigmentary mixture yields gray-black.

Ewald Hering, the physiologist, has this to say: "To medium or neutral gray corresponds that condition of the optic substance in which dissimilation — its consumption by vision — and assimilation — its regeneration — are equal, so that the quantity of optic substance remains the same. In other words, medium gray generates a state of complete equilibrium in the eye."

Hering shows that the eye and brain require medium gray, or become disquieted in its absence. If we view a white square on a black ground, and then look away, a black square appears as afterimage. If we look at a black square on a white ground, the afterimage is a white square. The state of equilibrium tends to reestablish itself in the eye. But if we look at a medium-gray square against a medium-gray background, no afterimage differing from the medium gray will appear. Thus medium gray matches the required equilibrium condition of our sense of sight.

Alterations in the optic substance correspond to subjective impressions. Harmony in our visual apparatus, then, would signify a psychophysical state of equilibrium in which dissimilation and assimilation of optic substance are equal. Neutral gray produces this state. I can mix such a gray from black and white, or from two complementary colors and white, or from several colors provided they contain the three primary colors yellow, red and blue in suitable proportions. In particular, any pair of complementary colors contains all three primaries:

red, green = red, (yellow and blue)
blue, orange = blue, (yellow and red)
yellow, violet = yellow, (red and blue)

So we can say that when a set of two or more colors contains yellow, red and blue in suitable proportions, the mixture will be gray. Yellow, red and blue may be substituted for the sum total of colors. Satisfaction of the eye requires this totality, and the eye is then in harmonic equilibrium.

Two or more colors are mutually harmonious if their mixture yields a neutral gray.

Any other color combinations, the mixture of which does not yield gray, are expressive, or discordant, in character. There are many great paintings having a one-sided, expressive intonation, and their color composition is not harmonious, in the sense here defined. Their one-sided, emphatic use of a particular color and its expression has an exciting and provocative effect. Thus not all color composition need be harmonious, and when Seurat said "Art is harmony," he was mistaking a means of art for its end.

Apart from the relative positions of the colors, of course, their quantitative proportion and their degrees of purity and brilliance are also important.

The basic principle of harmony is derived from the physiologically postulated rule of complementaries. In his Farbenlehre, Goethe writes on the subject of harmony and totality: "When the eye beholds a color, it is at once roused into activity, and its nature is, no less inevitably than unconsciously, to produce another color forthwith, which in conjunction with the given one encompasses the totality of the color circle. A particular color incites the eye, by a specific sensation, to strive for generality. In order, then, to realize this totality, in order to satisfy itself, the eye seeks, beside any color space, a colorless space wherein to produce the missing color. Here we have the fundamental rule of all color harmony."

Color harmony has also been discussed by Wilhelm Ostwald. He writes in his Primer of Colors, "Experience teaches that certain combinations of

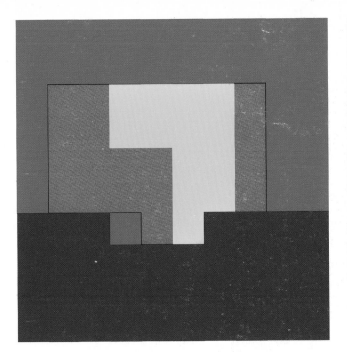  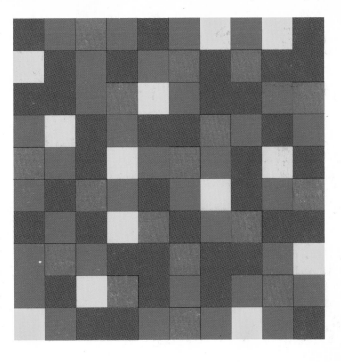

different colors are pleasing, others displeasing or indifferent. The question arises, what determines the effect? The answer is: Those colors are pleasing among which some regular, i. e. orderly, relationship obtains. Lacking this, the effect will be displeasing or indifferent. Groups of colors whose effect is pleasing, we call harmonious. So we can set up the postulate, Harmony = Order.

"To discover all possible harmonies, we must catalogue the possible instances of order in the color solid. The simpler the order, the more obvious or self-evident the harmony. Of such orders, we have found chiefly two, namely the color circles of equal shade (colors of like brilliance or like darkness) and the triangles of like hue (that is, the possible mixtures of a color with white or black). The circles of like shade yield harmonies of different hues, the triangles yield harmonies of like hue."

Where Ostwald says, "... colors whose effect is pleasing, we call harmonious," he implies a subjective criterion of harmony. But the concept of harmony should be removed from the realm of subjective attitude to that of objective principle, as I said previously.

Where Ostwald says, "Harmony = Order," and gives the color circles of equal shade and the color triangles of like hue as instances of order, he neglects the physiological laws of afterimage and simultaneity.

One essential foundation of any aesthetic color theory is the color circle, because that will determine the classification of colors. The color artist must work with pigments, and therefore his color classification must be constructed in terms of the mixing of pigments. That is to say, diametrally opposed colors must be complementary, mixing to yield gray. Thus in my color circle, the blue stands opposite to an orange; upon mixing, these colors give gray. In Ostwald's color circle, the blue stands opposite to a yellow, the pigmentary mixture yielding green. This fundamental difference in construction means that Ostwald's color circle is not serviceable to painting and the applied arts.

Having provided ourselves with a definition of harmony, let us proceed to the quantitave relationships among colors in harmonious composition. Goethe estimated the luminosities of the primary colors, and derived the following proportionality of areas:

$$\text{yellow} : \text{red} : \text{blue} = 3 : 6 : 8$$

We can make the general statement that all complementary pairs, all triads whose colors form equilateral or isosceles triangles in the twelve-member color circle, and all tetrads forming squares or rectangles, are harmonious (Fig. 6).

Figs. 7 and 8 illustrate the harmonious triad yellow/red/blue. Each of the three colors is presented in its typical and unmistakable character. Locating these hues on the 12-hue color circle, I get an equilateral triangle. This triad expresses the highest intensity and force of color. In the combination, each has its static effect; that is, the yellow acts as yellow, the red as red, the blue as blue. The eye demands no additional, completing colors, and the mixture of the three is a dark gray-black.

Figs. 9, 10, 11 show the harmonious tetrad yellow/red-orange/violet/blue-green.

Fig. 9 shows the four colors in their natural brilliances, occupying continuous areas of harmonious size.

In Fig. 10, the same colors have been broken up into many small squares. The four different brilliances produce instability, but the plastic force of the combination is more pronounced than in Fig. 9.

When I reduce the four degrees of brilliance to two, as in Fig. 11, the effect of the tetrad is two-dimensional. Between red-orange and blue-green/violet, a strong effect of cold-warm contrast develops. The static, fixed concord of Fig. 10 has been transformed, by reduction to two brilliances, into a new, suspensional timbre. If I reduced the four brilliances to one, painting all the colors as bright as yellow, the tone would again be entirely different.

Thus a harmonious combination can be varied in many ways.

The geometrical figures used — equilateral and isosceles triangles, square and rectangle — may of course be drawn from any given point on the circle. I can rotate them on the circle, thus replacing the triangle yellow/red/blue by the triangle yellow-orange/red-violet/blue-green, or the triangle orange/violet/green, or the triangle red-orange/blue-violet/yellow-green.

I can do the same with the other geometrical figures. Further discussion will be found in the section on harmonic variations.

12·13·14

SUBJECTIVE TIMBRE

In 1928, I was assigning harmonic color combinations to an art class. They were to be painted into complete circular areas, in sectors of unspecified size. I had not yet offered any definition of color harmony. After working away for twenty minutes or so, the class became very restless. I inquired what was the matter, and was told, "We all think that the combinations you assigned are not harmonious. We find them discordant and unpleasant."

I replied, "All right, let each of you paint whatever combinations he finds pleasant and harmonious."

The class quieted down at once, all eager to prove to me that my color combinations were wrong.

After an hour, I had the finished sheets spread out on the floor for inspection. Each student had painted several original, closely similar combinations on his sheet. But each student's work was very different from the others.

It was realized with astonishment that each had his own private conception of color harmony.

In closing this interesting session, I remarked, "The color combinations constructed as harmonious by each individual here represent individual subjective opinion. This is subjective color."

That early observation was to be followed by many more in ensuing years, and I have a large body of documentation in my possession today.

15 · 16 · 17

In order for this type of experiment to be successful, the painters must first have been sensitized to color generally. Without prior intensive study of the palette, and practice with brush and paints, reliable results cannot be obtained.

Experiments in subjective color should be initiated very carefully. Any suggestion that subjective color may reveal character or mode of thought and feeling should be avoided. Many people have inhibitions about showing themselves as they are. Anyone who works with color in his vocation is likely to have difficulty in discovering his subjective colors. Again, early attempts at color combinations are frequently wish fulfillments; subjects paint their complementary colors, or combinations in commercial vogue, instead of reflecting themselves.

Harmonies may be very close, with only two or three colors appearing, as light blue, medium gray, white and black, or dark brown-red, light brown-red and black, or yellow-green, yellow and black-brown, et cetera.

Again, their scope may be very wide – yellow, red, blue, in many degrees of saturation, also two or more pure colors in many different shades.

Between people with very narrow and very wide color scales, there are all conceivable intermediate positions.

There are subjective combinations in which one hue dominates quantitatively, all tones having accents of red, or yellow, or blue, or green, or violet, so that one is tempted to say that such-and-such a person sees the world in a red, yellow or blue light. It is as if he saw everything through tinted spectacles, perhaps with thoughts and feelings correspondingly colored.

In my studies of subjective color, I have found that not only the choice and juxtaposition of hues but also the size and orientation of areas may be highly characteristic. Some individuals orient all areas vertically; others stress the horizontal or diagonal. Orientation is a clue to mode of thought and feeling. Some individuals incline towards crisp and sharply bounded color areas, others to interpenetrating or blurred and haphazard patches. Individuals of the latter kind are not given to clear and simple thinking. They may be quite emotional and sentimentally disposed.

In any attempt to account for subjective color, we must attend to the most minute traits; but the essential factor is the "aura" of the person.

Some examples will illustrate different subjective color types.

Figs. 13, 14, the work of the young woman in Fig. 12, exhibit very pure colors, and a large number of clearly distinguished chromas. For her, the fundamental contrast is that of hue.

Figs. 16, 17 show the subjective tones of another student. Strong color seethes and clamors in the darker shades. Black is assigned a major role in the total concord, and pure colors are shot with black. Yellow is present in small amount, but glows with a pure ray in the somber whole. Blue-red is augmented towards violet, and contrasts with dull, complementary yellow-green. The strong, obscure chord displays a multitude of distinguishable shades, suggesting a lively and concentrated personality with intense feeling.

18·19

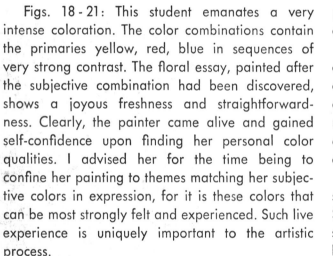

Figs. 18-21: This student emanates a very intense coloration. The color combinations contain the primaries yellow, red, blue in sequences of very strong contrast. The floral essay, painted after the subjective combination had been discovered, shows a joyous freshness and straightforwardness. Clearly, the painter came alive and gained self-confidence upon finding her personal color qualities. I advised her for the time being to confine her painting to themes matching her subjective colors in expression, for it is these colors that can be most strongly felt and experienced. Such live experience is uniquely important to the artistic process.

The construction of the painting personality should proceed from its subjectively given predispositions of form and color.

Knowledge of subjective timbres is of great importance in education and in art instruction. Education should naturally give every child the opportunity to evolve organically out of himself. Therefore educators must be able to recognize the aptitudes and potentialities of their pupils. Subjective color combinations are one key to identification of the individual's natural mode of thinking, feeling and doing. To help a student discover his subjective forms and colors is to help him discover himself. At first the difficulties may seem insurmountable. Yet let us trust in the immanent spirit of the individual.

The teacher's help should be offered sparingly, though certainly with sympathy and love. As a gardener prepares optimal conditions for the growth of his plants, so the educator should provide the child with favorable conditions of mental and physical growth. Such growth will then follow its own inherent directions and forces.

Art education involves two problems: to further and strengthen the learner's individual creative aptitudes, and to teach the general objective rules of form and color, supplemented by studies from nature. Here, too, individual aptitudes will be amplified and enlarged if the topics assigned are akin to the individual's subjective forms and colors.

The student of Fig. 15 should be assigned such subjects as Night, Light in a Dark Room, Autumn Storm, Burial, Grief, The Blues, etc. Her nature studies should be done in soft charcoal, or black and white pigments, with no geometrical delineation.

The girl of Fig. 12 needs assignments such as Springtime, Kindergarten, Baptism, Festival of Bright Flowers, Garden at Morning. Nature subjects should be vivid, without light-dark contrasts.

In other words, it is wrong to impose the same standard flower or figure studies on all students. Individual, subjectively slanted assignments are necessary so that students will be able to discover correct solutions intuitively. When a student is presented with themes "alien" to himself, he is forced to deal with them intellectually while as yet lacking the objective knowledge to do so.

After the student has grasped his own color principles, elementary exercises can be given in all the species of form and color contrast. It will then turn out that some individuals have a preference and flair for certain contrasts, and experience difficulty in handling others. Each student needs a grounding in universal principles, whether he likes it or not. They will generate within him natural tensions, prompting new creations.

20

21

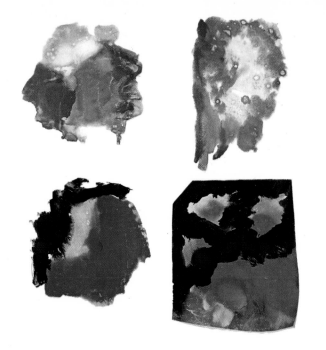
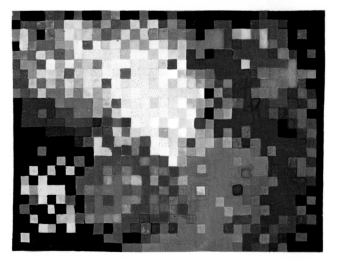

22 · 23 · 24

It is advisable to illustrate each contrast by analyses of paintings from the past and present. A learner benefits greatly when he encounters works that directly challenge and interest him. His favorite pictures become his masters, and he learns where he stands. One individual will feel drawn rather to the exponents of light-dark contrast, another to those of hue, of form, or of architectural composition. The strong colorism of the Expressionists, or the shape nihilism of the Tachistes, will enlist the preferences of some.

Figs. 22 - 28: On the first day of our work with subjective colors, this student painted patches of gray, blue, white and some red. I told her, "It seems to me you've already found your key colors." The next morning, she began to work with orange, black and purple. I was astonished, because to my mind, and in relation to this student's "aura", the new tones did not fit. I said, "Why waste your time? Didn't you find your colors yesterday?" She answered, "I have a feeling that these colors are just as important to me as the others." As her subjective colors show, she was an individual with exceptional breadth and depth of personality. All the principal colors, as well as black and white, are represented. It is no wonder that this student's exercises on the four seasons are so strongly defined; Figs. 25 - 28. Summer and autumn, in accord with the subjective attitude, show most power and life, but spring and winter too find intense coloristic expression. In her subjective color combinations, this student projected inner structures not manifest in her outward personality.

The total personality can rarely be quite comprehended in these concords; sometimes the physical, sometimes the mental or spiritual is dominant, or any of numerous composites. The emphasis varies with individual temperament and disposition.

Teachers, physicians and vocational counsellors can draw many valuable inferences from subjective colors.

One student's subjective colors were light violet, light blue, blue-gray, yellow, white, and a touch of black. His fundamental "tone" was hard, cold, and somewhat brittle. When he was discussing his choice of vocation with me, I suggested that he had a natural affinity for metals, particularly silver, and for glass. "You may be right, but I have decided to become a cabinetmaker," he rejoined. He did afterwards design furniture, and incidentally created the first modern steel chair. He ultimately became a highly successful architect in concrete and glass.

Another student's subjective color chords and compositions contained orange-brown, ocher, red-brown and some black. Green, blue, violet and gray tones were quite absent. When I asked him about his vocation, he said confidently, "I'm going to be a woodworker." He instinctively perceived his natural calling.

The subjective concords of a third student consisted of sonorous light-violet, yellowish and gold-brown tones. In their arrangement, these colors produced an effect of radiant splendor, suggesting great powers of concentration. The shading of warm yellow into light violet indicated a religious tendency of thinking. He served as sacristan to an important church, and was a consummate engraver in gold and silver besides.

A man cannot do his best except in an occupation that suits him constitutionally, and one for which he possesses the requisite aptitudes.

25

26

27

28

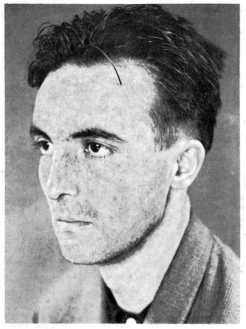

29 · 30 · 31

Figs. 30 - 35: A melancholy dusk of clouded colors embraces the light and brilliant combinations within the squares – concealed and captive. beauty incapable of emergence through the surrounding obstacles. The representations of the four seasons (Figs. 32 - 35) reveal the same melancholy. Spring, summer, autumn, winter are alike gray and sunless. The autumnal mood has a more general validity because its color expression approaches the subjective chord.

In Figs. 146 - 149, I have essayed an objective color characterization of the four seasons in as many different polytones. Comparison of these representations with the versions of Figs. 25 - 28 and 32 - 35 shows how great can be the influence of subjective attachment to certain colors.

It is worth mentioning that though I have diligently sought opinions on my color representations of the seasons, I have never yet found anyone who failed to identify each or any season correctly. This convinces me that above individual taste, there is a higher judgment in man, which, once appealed to, sustains what has general validity and overrules mere sentimental prejudice. This higher judgment is surely a faculty of the intellect. That is why well-disciplined color thinking and a knowledge of the potentialities of colors are necessary to save us from the one-sidedness and error of coloration informed by taste alone. If we can find objective rules of general validity in the realm of color, then it is our duty to study them.

Among painters, I perceive three different attitudes towards problems of color.

First there are the epigoni, having no coloration of their own but composing after the manner of their teachers or other exemplars.

The second group is that of the "originals" – those who paint as they themselves are. They compose according to their subjective timbre. Though the theme changes, the chromatic expression of their paintings remains the same.

Leonardo has reference to this group in his Trattato della Pittura: "How ridiculous are those painters who give their figures small heads because their own heads are small." What Leonardo was saying of subjective proportion, I would extend to subjective color.

The third group is that of the universalists – artists who compose from inclusive, objective considerations. Each of their compositions, according to the subject to be developed, has a different color treatment. That there should be but few painters in this group is understandable, for their subjective timbre must comprehend the entire color circle, and this happens rarely. Besides, they must possess high intelligence, admitting of a comprehensive philosophy.

If subjective timbre is significant of a person's inner being, then much of his mode of thought, feeling and action can be inferred from his color combinations. Intrinsic constitution and structures are reflected in the colors, which are generated by dispersion and filtration of the white light of life and by electromagnetic vibrations in the psycho-physiological medium of the individual.

When the individual dies, he blanches. His face and body lose color as the light of life is extinguished. The dead soulless matter of the corpse is devoid of chromatic emanation.

32

33

34

35

Interpretation of subjective color combinations is not to be based on the several chromas and their expressional values alone. The timbre as a whole is of first importance, then the placement of the colors relative to each other, their directions, brilliances, clarity or turbidity, their proportions, textures and rhythmic relationships.

Decorators and designers sometimes tend to be guided by their own subjective color propensities. This may lead to misunderstandings and disputes, where one subjective judgment collides with another. For the solution of many problems, however, there are objective considerations that outweigh subjective preferences. Thus a meat market may be decorated in light green and blue-green tones, so that the various meats will appear fresher and redder. Confectionery shows to advantage in light orange, pink, white, and accents of black, stimulating an appetite for sweets. If a commercial artist were to design a package for coffee bearing yellow and white stripes, or one with blue polka-dots for spaghetti, he would be wrong because these form and color features are in conflict with the theme.

Accordingly, gardeners are daily concerned with important problems of form and color. They observe the growth of plants, their shapes and proportions, and the colors of blossoms, foliage and fruit. The soil, surrounding vegetation, rocks, and conditions of light and shade must receive due consideration if plantings are to produce hoped-for effects. One cannot simply choose one's favorite species and colors of flowers. It would be wrong to plant blue larkspur against a brown wooden fence, or yellow flowers in front of a white stone wall, because these backgrounds would detract from the color effect.

Florists are rigidly dependent on the season and on the varieties available from time to time. Despite these restrictions, they must continually find objectively correct combinations for all sorts of occasions, and they cannot do so on the basis of personal taste alone. The floral décor for a wedding should be joyful; besides passionate reds and pinks, any vivid hues may be included. For a christening, one would never choose dark blue or dark green, but deliberately prefer light, delicate, small blossoms, in colors of white, light blue, pink, light yellow, as well as light green. Called upon to supply floral decorations for the anniversary of an association, the florist would arrange strong colors and large blossoms in ceremonial, rather impersonal combinations, including distinctive green leaf forms, the whole to express disciplined but festive power.

Salespeople whose customers are sensitive to color will be more successful if they try to understand their customers' tastes rather than to impose their own. Every woman should know what colors are becoming to her; these will always be her subjective colors and their complements. When a customer is looking for a certain hue, one needs to know what other colors may strengthen, weaken, or simultaneously modify it. Brightly colored merchandise should not be left within the buyer's field of vision, because it may exert powerful simultaneous influences. For the same reason, salesrooms where the colors of goods are to be appreciated should always be done in neutral grays.

Fashion executives require familiarity with the general, objectively valid principles of form and color. Several times a year, the fashion designer is expected to come up with a new line in the fashionable colors. If these are close to his subjective colors, he will easily discover the tints and shades he needs. His line will be convincing and successful. But if the hues required by fashion are counter to his subjective colors, he will find his task ungrateful and laborious.

If an interior decorator's personal spectrum is dominated by blue-gray, he will "naturally" tend to do all sorts of interiors in blue-gray tones, these being particularly satisfying to himself. Clients who are chromatically "related" to him will be pleased; but those who are attuned to orange, or green, will find their surroundings uncongenial and will feel ill-at-ease.

Nowadays, architects frequently put up great blocks of dwellings in uniform colors. They should realize that only people of corresponding color sense will enjoy these quarters, and that all others will be more or less repelled. Uncongenial colors may constitute a severe stress upon sensitive individuals. Is not generality of well-being a more important aim than aesthetic unity?

These examples all go to show that subjective taste cannot suffice for the solution of all color problems. Knowledge of objective principles is essential to the correct evaluation and use of colors.

Constructive color theory embraces the principles of color effects insofar as they can be derived empirically.

When Rainer Maria Rilke one day asked Rodin, "Cher maître, how would you describe the creative process, from the inception of a project?" Rodin replied: "First I experience an intense feeling, which gradually becomes more concrete and urges me to give it plastic shape. Then I proceed to plan and design. At last, when it comes to execution, I once more abandon myself to feeling, which may prompt me to modify the plan."

Cézanne said of himself, "Je vais au développement logique de ce que je vois dans la nature." *)

Matisse, seemingly guided mainly by his own feeling, made little sketches of projected paintings, and indicated the selection and distribution of colors in writing, before beginning to paint. In other words, he too, like Rodin and other masters, devised a rationally calculated composition, which he would afterwards use or reject according to his subjective feeling during the course of the work (Fig. 36).

Any calculated plan, then, will not be the ruling factor. Intuitive feeling is superior to it, navigating the realm of the irrational and metaphysical, not subject to number. Deliberate intellectual construction is the "conveyance" that carries us to the portals of this new reality.

In order to learn the objective principles of color, take brush in hand and reproduce the charts and exercises in this book. The figures show only elementary examples, and the beginning colorist must do a great many more exercises if he is to progress beyond the theoretical. As a rule, I give only one instance of each color effect. The student should work out his own plates for the other colors.

36

*) I proceed to a logical development of what I see in nature.

By way of introduction to color design, let us develop the 12-hue color circle from the primaries – yellow, red and blue (Fig. 37). As we know, a person with normal vision can identify a red that is neither bluish, nor yellowish; a yellow that is neither greenish, nor reddish; and a blue that is neither greenish, nor reddish. In examining each color, it is important to view it against a neutral-gray background.

The primary colors must be defined with the greatest possible accuracy. We place them in an equilateral triangle with yellow at the top, red at the lower right and blue at the lower left.

About this triangle we circumscribe a circle, in which we inscribe a regular hexagon. In the isosceles triangles between adjacent sides of the hexagon, we place three mixed colors, each composed of two primaries. Thus we obtain the secondary colors:

yellow + red = orange
yellow + blue = green
red + blue = violet

The three secondary colors have to be mixed very carefully. They must not lean towards either primary component. You will note that it is no easy task to obtain the secondaries by mixture. Orange must be neither too red, nor too yellow; violet neither too red, nor too blue; and green must be neither too yellow, nor too blue.

Now, at a convenient radius outside the first circle, let us draw another circle, and divide the ring between them into twelve equal sectors. In this ring, we repeat the primaries and secondaries at their appropriate locations, leaving a blank sector between every two colors.

In these blank sectors, we then paint the tertiary colors, each of which results from mixing a primary with a secondary, as follows:

yellow + orange = yellow-orange
red + orange = red-orange
red + violet = red-violet
blue + violet = blue-violet
blue + green = blue-green
yellow + green = yellow-green

Thus we have constructed a regular 12-hue color circle in which each hue has its unmistakable place. The sequence of the colors is that of the rainbow or natural spectrum.

Newton obtained a continuous color circle of this kind by supplementing the spectral hues with purple, between red and violet. So the color circle is an artificially augmented spectrum.

The twelve hues are evenly spaced, with complementary colors diametrically opposite each other.

One can accurately visualize any of these twelve hues at any time, and any intermediate tones are easily located.

I think it is a waste of time for the colorist to practice making 24-hue, or 100 hue, color circles. Can any painter, unaided, visualize Color No. 83 of a 100-hue circle?

Unless our color names correspond to precise ideas, no useful discussion of colors is possible. I must see my twelve tones as precisely as a musician hears the twelve tones of his chromatic scale.

Delacroix kept a color circle mounted on a wall of his studio, each color labeled with possible combinations. The Impressionists, Cézanne, Van Gogh, Signac, Seurat and others, esteemed Delacroix as an eminent colorist. Delacroix, rather than Cézanne, is the founder of the tendency, among modern artists, to construct works upon logical, objective color principles, so achieving a heightened degree of order and truth.

We speak of contrast when distinct differences can be perceived between two compared effects. When such differences attain their maximum degree, we speak of diametrical or polar contrasts. Thus, large-small, white-black, cold-warm, in their extremes, are polar contrasts. Our sense organs can function only by means of comparisons. The eye accepts a line as long when a shorter line is presented for comparison. The same line is taken as short when the line compared with it is longer. Color effects are similarly intensified or weakened by contrast.

The physiological problem of contrast effects lies in the special field of aesthesiology, and will not be taken up here.

When we survey the characteristics of 'color effects, we can detect seven different kinds of contrast. These are so different that each will have to be studied separately. Each is unique in character and artistic value, in visual, expressive and symbolic effect, and together they constitute the fundamental resource of color design.

Goethe, Bezold, Chevreul and Hölzel have noted the significance of the various color contrasts. Chevreul devoted an entire work to "Contraste Simultané". However, a systematic and practical introduction to the special effects of color contrast, with exercises, has been lacking. Such an exploration of the color contrasts is an essential part of my course of instruction.

The seven kinds of color contrast are the following:

1. Contrast of hue

2. Light-dark contrast

3. Cold-warm contrast

4. Complementary contrast

5. Simultaneous contrast

6. Contrast of saturation

7. Contrast of extension

38

39

Contrast of hue is the simplest of the seven. It makes no great demands upon color vision, because it is illustrated by the undiluted colors in their most intense luminosity. Some obvious combinations are: yellow/red/blue; red/blue/green; blue/yellow/violet; yellow/green/violet/red; violet/green/blue/orange/black.

Just as black-white represents the extreme of light-dark contrast, so yellow/red/blue is the extreme instance of contrast of hue (Fig. 38). At least three clearly differentiated hues are required. The effect is always tonic, vigorous and decided. The intensity of contrast of hue diminishes as the hues employed are removed from the three primaries.

Thus orange, green and violet are weaker in character than yellow, red and blue, and the effect of tertiary colors is still less distinct.

When the single colors are separated by black or white lines, their individual characters emerge more sharply (Fig. 39). Their interaction and mutual influences are suppressed to some extent. Each hue acquires an effect of reality, concreteness. Though the triad yellow/red/blue represents the strongest contrast of hue, all pure, undiluted colors of course can participate in this contrast.

Contrast of hue assumes a large number of entirely new expressive values when the brilliances are varied. In the same way, the quantitative proportions of yellow, red and blue may be modified. Variations are numberless, and so are the corresponding expressive potentialities. Whether black and white are included as elements of the palette will depend on subject matter and individual preference. As was shown in Figs. 2 - 4, white weakens the luminosity of adjacent hues and darkens them; black causes them to seem lighter. Hence white and black may be powerful elements of color composition.

The same exercises might be worked out in patches of color without preassigned shapes. However, this procedure would involve hazards. The student would start experimenting with shapes instead of studying color areas and tensions. He would draw outlines, and this practice is hostile to color design and should be strictly avoided. In most exercises, we use simple stripe or checkerboard patterns.

In exercises like Figs. 38 and 39, the colors combined are placed in rectangular fields, and changes in relative size can be made horizontally.

Fig. 40 shows a checkerboard arrangement. The student must lay out the colors in two dimensions, and this develops the feeling for areal tensions. Once the combinations on the pattern of Figs. 38, 39 have been evolved, the learner can quickly discover the color selections for such exercises as shown in Fig. 40.

Very interesting studies are obtained if one hue is given the principal role, and others are used in small quantities, merely as accents. Emphasizing one color enhances expressive character. After each geometrical exercise is carried out, free compositions in the same kind of contrast should be attempted.

There are many subjects that can be painted in contrast of hue. The significance of this contrast involves the interplay of primeval luminous forces. The undiluted primaries and secondaries always have a character of aboriginal cosmic splendor as well as of concrete actuality. Therefore they serve equally well to portray a celestial coronation or a mundane still life.

Contrast of hue is found in the folk art of peoples everywhere. Gay embroidery, costume and pottery testify to primitive delight in colorful effects. In the illuminated manuscripts of the Middle Ages, contrast of hue was used in manifold variations, often not from motives of aesthetic necessity but out of sheer pleasure in decorative invention.

Contrast of hue is dominant also in early stained glass, its primordial force actually asserting itself over the plastic form of architecture. Stefan Lochner, Fra Angelico and Botticelli are among painters who have based compositions on contrast of hue.

Perhaps the grandest example of its significant use is Grünewald's "Resurrection" (Plate XXVII), where this contrast displays all of its universalistic power of expression.

So in Botticelli's "Lamentation" (in the Pinakothek, Munich), contrast of hue serves to characterize the all-embracing grandeur of the scene. The totality of hues symbolizes the cosmic significance of the epochal event.

Here we see that the expressive potentialities of one and the same color contrast may be widely diverse. Contrast of hue may alike express boisterous joviality, profound grief, earthy simplicity and cosmic universality.

Among the moderns, Matisse, Mondrian, Picasso, Kandinsky, Léger and Miró have frequently composed in this mode. Matisse especially uses it in still-life and figure paintings. A good example is the portrait "Le Collier d'Ambre," painted in the pure colors of red, yellow, green, blue, red-violet, white and black. This combination expressively characterizes a young, sensitive and clever woman.

The Blauer Reiter painters Kandinsky, Franz Marc and August Macke, worked in contrast of hue almost exclusively during their early period.

Out of the wealth of examples available, I have chosen four for discussion.

40

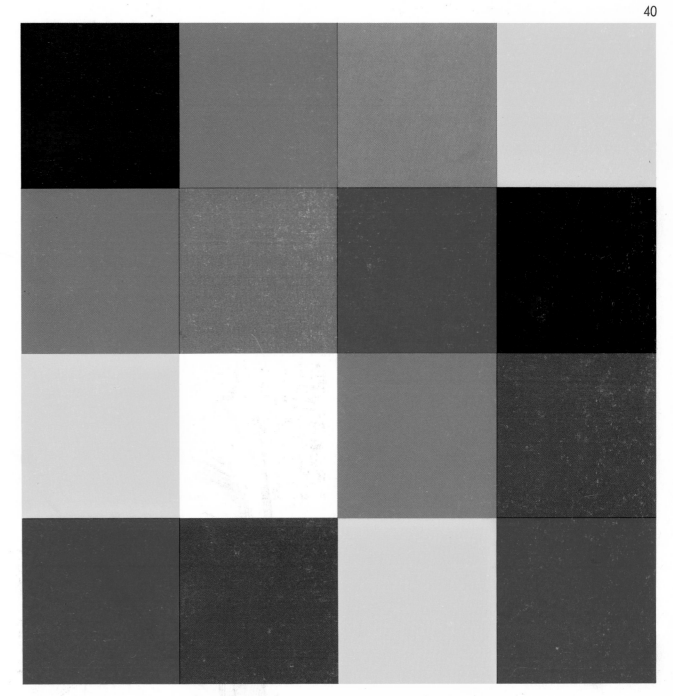

All the paintings in this eleventh-century manuscript, preserved in the Bibliothèque Nationale at Paris, are done in contrast of hue. This lends the entire work an abstract, supra-real expression, befitting the theme of the Apocalypse. In the illustration shown, three colors, yellow, red and blue, are strikingly emphasized in five horizontal stripes. A fourth principal color, green, is added in the architecture and the two figures. It is interesting how the rhythmic outlines are sometimes black and sometimes red, producing special accents between red and green, red and blue, red and yellow. The horizontal yellow/red/blue articulation contrasts with the vertical figures, while the rhythmic lines in the garments and wings provide a contrast of texture with the plain areas of the background. Likewise, the columns and the roofs have contrary scaly textures.

If we compare this illustration with the others, we note the great significance of the relative areas of colors; here, yellow strongly dominates the effect. Symbolically, yellow denotes intellect, knowledge, wisdom, or light and enlightenment. The blue-winged angel, issuing from the blue, is green and red. His red dress signifies fiery activity, while St. John, the recipient of the message, appears in passive blue and green. The faces are white, giving an abstract effect beneath the black of the hair. The seven towers stand for the seven churches in the seven cities to which John is to dispatch the message. As John's whole prophecy represents future events in symbolic images, so the forms and colors in these illuminations are to be understood symbolically. No aesthetic prettiness, but grandiose truths, are announced by this painter through the elementary colors yellow, red, blue and green.

Our Plate XVI, "Satan and the Locusts," is from the same manuscript, and will be discussed under the heading of composition.

AECCLA EPHESI.

A INCIP EXPLANATIO SUPRA SCRIPTAE STORIAE ET AECCLAE IN LIBRO SCDO
Angelo aephesi aecclae scribe: Sub unius appellatione angli omnium scorum numeru signat Ephesi aute
qd e voluntas sive consilu meu Catholica ut supis memoraui narrat aecctameu sit loqui manfestet Haec dicit

This painting is divided into two main parts by a film of white cloud, which separates the celestial from the terrestrial world. The latter, painted in grayish tones, is divided into the upper and the nether world, with the saved on the left and the damned on the right.

In the center of the upper world stands a gigantic crucifix. It rises high into the dull blue aerial ocean. All forms in the terrestrial world are tiny and insignificant in relation to the heroic central group of God the Father, Christ, and Mary, in heaven. These three figures are emphasized by overwhelming stature. This effect is intensified by contrast with the size of the crucifix. The crucifix is enormous relative to earthly cities, and minute as measured by the celestial scale. It is the only feature joining the two worlds. This relationship expresses the universal significance of Christ's mission.

The main central group is separated from the ocean by the white arc of Mary's robe. This arc provides a contrast of form with the horizontal layer of white cloud. The circle and its arc symbolize the heavenly infinite, contrasting with the square, or the horizontal and vertical, representing earthly limitation. The heavenly arc is repeated in the white clouds beneath the mantles of the Father and the Son. To the left and right of the main group, the saints are represented in vivid colors and medium proportions. The three different scales, from the small temporal world to the great central group, and the intermediate size of the saints, connote a hierarchy of being.

A white ermine facing marks off the luminous blue of the Virgin's mantle from the dull blue of the ocean. Her gold brocade gown rises in a stiff, as if inanimate, form. Only her face and hands seem lifelike; her body is utterly unreal, and largely eclipsed on either side by the mantles of the crowning Persons.

Above Mary's head hovers the white dove of the Holy Spirit. A perpendicular line drawn from the crucifix would intersect the cross on the dove's nimbus at the upper edge of the picture.

God the Father and God the Son are enthroned to the right and left of this line. The two figures are nearly symmetrical. The only asymmetrical feature is the gold brocade border descending Christ's robe. It parallels Mary's brocade dress, indicating the corporeal bond of Mother and Son.

This central group is encircled by a heavenly host depicted in an orange tone. Above them shines yellow celestial light, continued on either side down to the blue sea and causing the central group to appear flat and incorporeal as if floating in the light. These yellow areas have the same function as the blue angels in each upper corner of the picture, which repeat the blue color of the Virgin's mantle and thus intensify the floating effect of the central group.

In the composition of this monumental painting, Charonton used the colors gold, orange, red, blue, green, white and gray. At the top, he begins with yellow, materialized celestial light. This condenses into darker orange, the might of the heavenly hosts. Contrasting with this transcendental world is the red of the mantles of Father and Son, descending out of divine love – symbolized by red – into the intermediate world, to crown the Virgin. Their garments are white. Mary's gold brocade dress signifies ennobled, purified corporeality, and the blue of her robe expresses passivity and pious resignation. The groups of saints to the left and right of the picture display clear, luminous, colorful life. The terrestrial world seems gray and joyless. Only at the extreme left and right, two structures appear in light red, suggesting that here mankind has communion with the divine sphere.

This painting by Charonton evidences the same universality of artistic thinking that we see in Grünewald.

Plate III
Paul de Limbourg, May-Day Excursion, from the
manuscript "Les Très Riches Heures du Duc de
Berry," 1410.
Chantilly, Musée Condé

In 1409, at the age of seventy, the Duke of
Berry commissioned the foremost illuminator of his
time, Paul de Limbourg, to execute a Book of Hours.
The Duke was personally concerned that only the
best and whitest parchment, the purest gold, and
the costliest blue pigment — powdered lapis lazuli
— should be used. It was an obsession with him to
have work of the utmost beauty in form and color,
and in the noblest materials. Brother to Philip the
Bold, he affected Burgundian elegance at his court,
and his possessions of jewelry, gold plate, costly
stuffs and tapestries betokened the luxury of the
age. So the miniatures for the Book of Hours
portray the lands, castles and manors of the Duke,
the life and labor of his peasants, and the feasts
and diversions of the gentry. However, before the
book was completed, the Duke died penniless, his
perfectionism in externals having exhausted his
means.

For us, these miniatures by Paul de Limbourg
represent the utmost of perfection and beauty ever
achieved in the genre. Our plate shows the calendar
page for the month of May. The picture represents
a gay company of notables in holiday attire and
leafy garlands, riding out a-Maying. It was custom-
ary on this occasion to present green-tinted
costumes to the young girls. The light green is
expressive of new spring, and the pigment was
rare and costly. The ultramarine blue mantles of
the riders are also strikingly beautiful. In the
center of the cavalcade rides a nobleman in
extravagant parti-colored dress, white and black
on the right, red and gold on the left. Fashion
followed Italian models. Sumptuous gold-embroi-
dered silks and satins, trimmed with pearls, precious
stones and furs, lent pomp to the celebration. The
representation of such luxury was not considered
inappropriate in a prayer book.

All this blaze of color is organized into a cool
and elegant symphony. The composition of black,
white, gray, blue, red, green, and yellow gold, is
in perfect contrast of hue. Rich polytonality
lends the entire scene a gay, lively and strong
expression.

Mondrian's original contribution to modern painting is momentous. His choice of theme never varies. His paintings employ two elementary resources, contrast of proportion and contrast of hue. Among the three categories of shape – square, circle, triangle – he selected the square, the form determined by horizontal and vertical direction. He subdivides the picture area with straight lines. The quantitative proportions of the resulting areas assume a peculiarly independent life. Small configurations gain great significance by their placement in the field, while large forms recede and seem as if congealed. High sensitivity to proportion is required to organize all areas of a painting into a balanced whole.

In his later pictures, Mondrian confined himself to the fundamental colors yellow, red, blue, white and black. Each of these colors has its unique character and special weight. The position of each color is very important, and so is its orientation, horizontal or vertical. As in "Composition 1928," Mondrian can create a stable equilibrium with a small blue area and a large white area, or intensify the whole with a slender horizontal yellow area at the bottom. Great stability and clarity are achieved by dividing the field with broad black lines. The separating black causes each color to appear isolated and concrete. Mondrian's forms and colors are used without expressional or symbolic intent. His feeling for clean design leads him to an unadorned, visually strong, geometrical, elemental realism of form and color.

The following statement is Mondrian's own: "The life of civilized man today is turning aside, little by little, from natural things, to become increasingly an abstract life. As natural (external) things become more and more automatic, real interest, as we see, turns rather to things internal. The truly modern man's life is determined neither in a purely materialistic way nor purely by feeling. Rather, it assumes the guise of a more autonomic life of the human spirit grown aware of itself."

Day and night, light and darkness — this polarity is of fundamental significance in human life and nature generally. The painter's strongest expressions of light and dark are the colors white and black. The effects of black and white are in all respects opposite, with the realm of grays and chromatic colors between them. The phenomena of light and dark, both among white, black and gray, and among pure colors, should be thoroughly studied, for they yield valuable guides to our work.

Black velvet is perhaps the blackest black, and baryta is the purest white. There is only one maximal black and one maximal white, but an indefinitely large number of light and dark grays, forming a continuous scale between white and black.

The number of distinguishable shades of gray depends on the sensitivity of the eye and the response threshold of the observer. This threshold can be lowered by practice, increasing the number of perceptible gradations. A uniformly gray, lifeless surface can be awakened to mysterious activity by extremely minute modulations of shading. This very important factor in painting and drawing requires extreme sensitivity to tonal differences.

Neutral gray is a characterless, indifferent, achromatic color, very readily influenced by contrasting shade and hue. It is mute, but easily excited to thrilling resonances. Any color will instantly transform gray from its neutral, achromatic state to a complementary color effect corresponding mathematically to the activating color. This transformation occurs subjectively, in the eye, not objectively in the colors themselves. Gray is a sterile neuter, dependent on its neighboring colors for life and character. It attenuates their force and mellows them. It will reconcile violent oppositions by absorbing their strength and thereby, vampire-like, assuming a life of its own.

Delacroix objected to gray for this reason, as injurious to the power of color.

Gray may be mixed from black and white, or from yellow, red, blue and white, or from any pair of complementary colors.

Fig. 41 represents a regular series of grays from white to black, in twelve steps. It is important to space the steps evenly. The gray of medium brilliance should be in the center of the scale. Each individual step should be perfectly uniform and spotless, with neither a light nor a dark line between it and its neighbors. Similar scales of brilliance can be prepared for any chromatic color. In the blue scale, blue is darkened with black down to blue-black, and lightened with white up to blue-white.

These exercises serve to sharpen the student's sensitivity to shading. The twelve steps are not intended, as in music, to represent a system of "equal temperament." In the art of color, not only precise intervals but inappreciable transitions, comparable to the glissando in music, may be important vehicles of expression. (See Fig. 57.)

The following exercises are intended to enlarge comprehension of light-dark contrast.

Fig. 42: Certain grays are selected from the scale of grays obtained, and they are then arranged in four equal areas to form a composition. When five or six such compositions have been completed, they are rated comparatively. It is soon realized that some are good and convincing, others poor or false. This very simple exercise will assess a talent for chiaroscuro.

Fig. 43 shows the development of a light-dark combination upon a checkered surface. This composition may be lightened or darkened as a whole; the main point is to cultivate vision and perception of light-dark gradations and their contrasts.

Fig. 44: When an understanding of white-gray-black gradation has been gained, contrast of proportion or quantity may be added to light-dark contrast. Two contrasts then operate simultaneously. Contrast of proportion comprises large-small, long-short, wide-narrow, thick-thin. Let us follow out some simple exercises in problems of proportion. These will also illustrate the relationship of shape to its negative or inverse. In black-and-white print, we think of the black area as positive and the white as its negative.

41

42

44

43

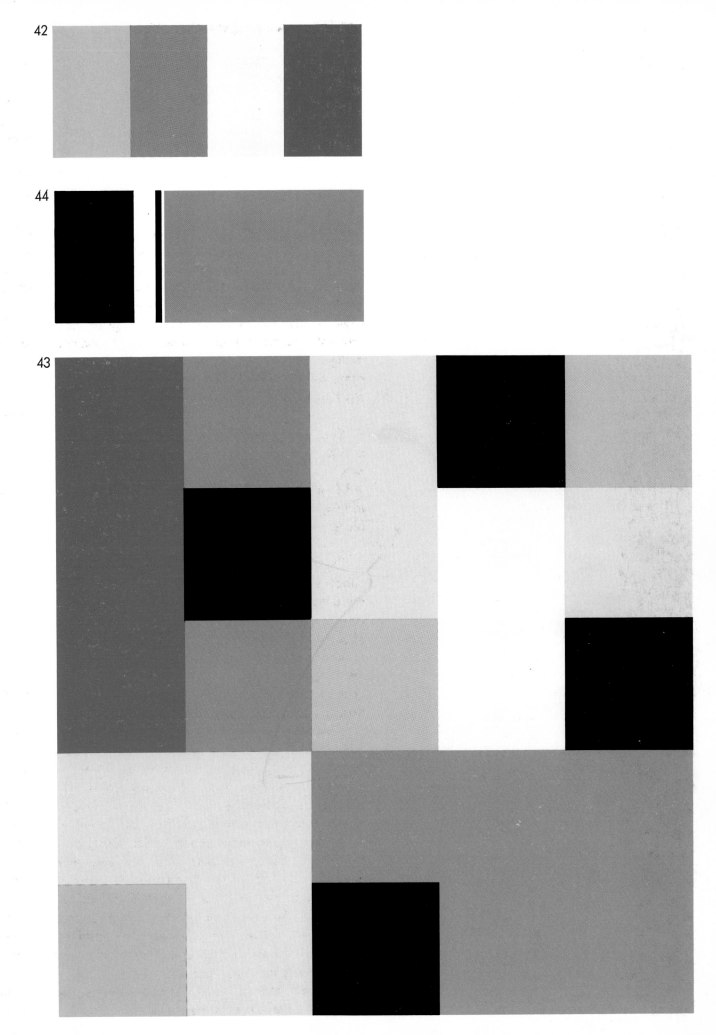

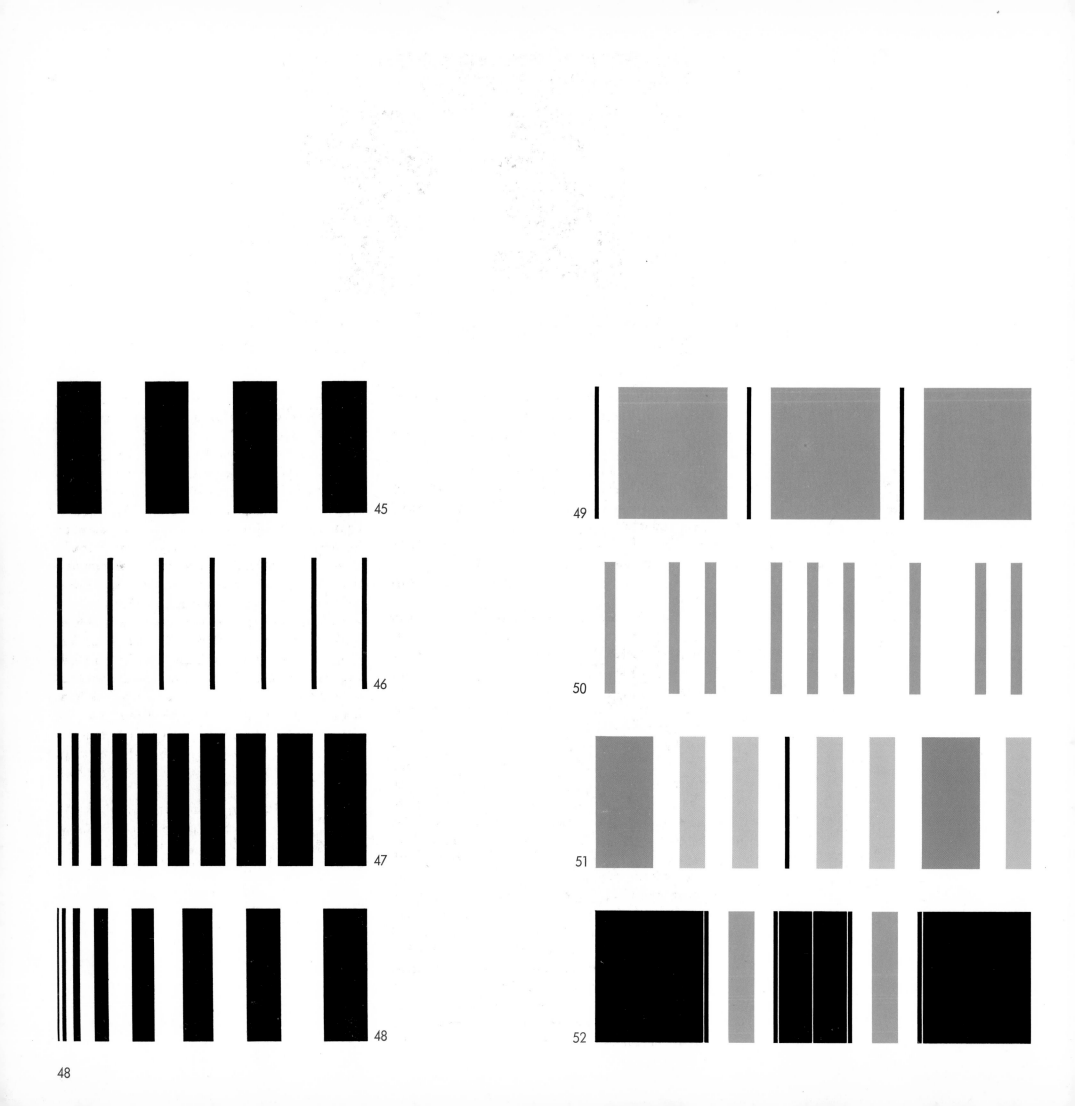

45

46

47

48

49

50

51

52

53

Fig. 45: The black and white widths are equal; contrast of proportion is not operative.

Fig. 46: Positive narrow, negative wide. Strong contrast of proportion.

Fig. 47: Positive graduated, negative constant.

Fig. 48: Positive and negative both graduated.

Fig. 49: Triad, gray/white/black, strong contrast of proportion.

Fig. 50: Gray and white in three rhythmically related groups.

Fig. 51: Tetrad, white/light-gray/dark-gray/black.

Fig. 52: Triad. Grouping is essential to a clear contrast of proportion. Clear distinctions of light and dark are also important. Repetition of the narrow white and black lines interconnects the groups.

Of course, infinite variations on each of these themes are possible.

Much European and Asian art is constructed upon pure light-dark contrast. Chinese and Japanese ink drawing is an outstanding example. The technique of this art stems from the art of writing in these countries, where ideographic characters, representing a wealth of forms, are made with the brush. Their semantically and rhythmically correct execution requires a repertory of many different manual motions. Sense of form, rhythmic feeling and relaxed attentiveness are necessary to "correct" brushwork. In China and Japan, writing is a fine art. "When an archer has thoroughly sighted his target, poised his body, grasped his bow firmly, and aimed accurately, the arrow will almost certainly hit the mark. So with the calligrapher: with the mind concentrated, the body upright and balanced, the brush vertical, the dot or stroke should fall exactly on the appointed place." (Chiang Yee, "Chinese Calligraphy," Harvard University Press.)

Fig. 53 shows two Chinese characters. The rhythmic harmony of these symbols, their structure, their rich contrast of forms, abstract and organically integrated, are exquisitely beautiful. This effect is made possible by a perfect equilibrium between the black brush strokes and the white intervals. When we recall that these characters were executed cursively, we can appreciate the harmonic powers and inner composure of the calligrapher.

This writing proceeds from an inward automatism. After endless practice, the strokes at last flow effortlessly from the brush; and in the same way, the Chinese or Japanese painter practices the lexicon of nature until he can reproduce it at will. This discipline presupposes mental concentration and physical relaxation. Meditation as practiced particularly in Ch'an, or Zen, Buddhism provides the foundation of this training of mind and body. Accordingly, many monks of this sect are to be found among the great artists in black and white. They did not engage in meditation in order to become great painters; they worked with the brush as an aid to meditative internalization.

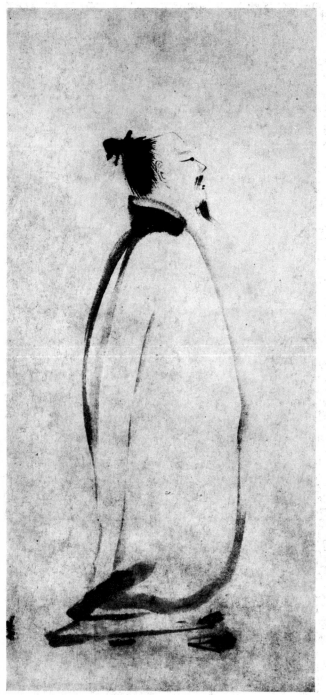

54

Fig. 54 shows the poet Li Po as portrayed by Liang K'ai.

One of the greatest geniuses of this medium was Liang K'ai, who lived about the first half of the thirteenth century. Each of his pictures is different from the others. This representation of the poet in a few black and gray lines and patches is unique in painting. Spots of highly differentiated size and a few spare strokes evoke a distinguished figure, striding forth with distant gaze. Each element is most delicately attuned to the total effect. Liang K'ai was a monk of the Ch'an sect.

55

Fig. 55 shows a detail of a mountain landscape by Sesshû.

To create this subtle group, the painter used only diluted ink in varying tones. The light open spots are of equal importance with the gray and black areas.

Soft gray tones are set off by hard black strokes and patches as contrasts. Contrasts of light and dark, hard and soft, and horizontal, vertical and diagonal direction, form a complex and abstract harmony in which each element is generated out of a concentrated internal process, automatic, uninhibited, and yet controlled. This strength and freshness, so spontaneously created, must have resulted from intense, sincere feeling. The Japanese painter Sesshû (1420 - 1507) made several visits to China, where he studied Ch'an as well as painting.

Other media of light-dark expression are the woodcut, copperplate and etching. The artist, by shading and hatching, can produce extremely differentiated gradations of light and dark. Rembrandt's etchings cover a very wide range of subject matter. As is not surprising, he also executed pen-and-ink and brush drawings in masterful chiaroscuro, often rivaling the suggestive power and clarity of East Asian work.

Fig. 56: Rembrandt, Dr. Faustus, etching.

By means of different positions of lines, the technique of etching is able to produce extraordinarily fine differentiations of shading, and therefore very lively and diversified areas. Though this etching of Rembrandt's is polytonic in light and dark, yet the many tones are grouped on two main levels of light and darkness. The questing Faustus emerges clearly as the insatiable intellect, from the antithesis of shadings. His penetration into the depths of life is dramatically visualized in the spatial tension between his figure and the luminous apparition at the window.

56

Fig. 57: Seurat, Le Noeud, study.

In his numerous sketches, Seurat explored light-dark gradations most conscientiously. In this example, the standing figure is outlined with one light and one dark line of contrast, and its plastic form is modeled with light and dark areas in very subtle transitions. The way the shading is developed from the shoulder highlight gradually to the deep tone of the baseline, and the latter linked to the tones of the dark background, is authoritative. The fall of the black bow and its linkage to the dark tone of the dress also show conscious mastery of light-dark composition.

Seurat's drawings, like his paintings, give one the feeling that he is devoting thought to each pinpoint in order to evoke the most delicate of shadings.

57

Thus far, we have considered light-dark contrast only in the range of black, white and gray. The light-dark evaluation of chromatic colors and their relationships to the achromatic colors – black, white and gray – is far more complicated. The domain of grays extends between white and black, just as the world of colors burns between light and darkness.

Gradations and brilliancies of achromatic colors are easily distinguished, and so are those within each chromatic hue. Difficulties arise when gradations of unlike hues are to be compared. It is most important to be able to identify colors of equal brilliance accurately. The following exercise will help to develop this ability.

In a checkerboard array, we place yellow or red or blue. We are then required to add colors having the same amount of light or dark as the given color. We make a point of using yellowish, bluish and reddish hues on each attempt. Brilliance must not be confused with the saturation, or purity, of the colors.

Special difficulties are presented by cold and warm colors. Cold colors seem transparent, weightless, and are commonly rendered too light, whereas the warm hues, because of their opacity, tend to be rendered too dark. The exercise of painting all the hues in the same brilliance as yellow is difficult because it is not immediately realized how brilliant yellow is. It is similarly difficult to render yellow as dark as red or blue. Shading and dilution necessarily deprive brilliant yellow of its yellowness; this naturally disinclines many people to darken yellow.

How these principles have been used by eminent painters may be seen in Plates V, XI, XX and XXIII.

Equality of light or dark relates colors to each other, tying or bracketing them together. Light-dark contrast between them is extinguished. This is an invaluable resource of artistic design.

In the color sphere, Figs. 112 and 113, both the chromatic colors of the twelve-hue color circle and the achromatic colors are represented. Contrary to the chromatic colors, the achromatic colors produce an effect of the categorical, rigid, incorruptible and abstract. They are in antithesis to the vibrant complexity of the chromatic colors. Yet it is possible for the achromatic colors to acquire a borrowed chromatic effect. By simultaneous contrast (Figs. 80 - 85), a neighboring hue may induce an achromatic gray to look like its complementary hue. When achromatic colors occur in a composition and adjoin chromatic colors of like brilliance, they lose their achromatic character.

If the achromatic colors are to retain their condition of abstraction, the chromatic colors must be of different brilliance. In a composition where whites, blacks and grays are used as means for abstract effect, there should be no chromatic colors matching them in brilliance, or simultaneous contrast will activate the neutrals. When gray is used as an active component in a color composition, then the adjoining chromatic tone must match the gray in brilliance.

The Impressionists were interested in this active function of grays, whereas constructionist and concrete painters use black, white and gray abstractly.

The problems of chromatic light-dark contrast are illustrated by Fig. 58. The twelve equidistant steps from white to black as developed in Fig. 41 have been repeated for each of the twelve hues of the color circle, in brilliances equal to the corresponding grays. We see that the pure yellow answers to the fourth step. Orange is at the sixth step, red at the eighth, blue at the ninth, and violet at the tenth step in the scale of grays. The chart shows saturated yellow to be the lightest of the pure colors, and violet the darkest.

Thus yellow must be muted from the fifth step on, in order to match the darker tones of the gray scale. Pure red and blue are at a lower level, leaving few steps to black, but many on the way to white. Each admixture of black or white reduces the vividness of a hue.

Along any horizontal row of the chart, all squares should be of the same brilliance as the corresponding gray.

If we prepare a sequence of as many as eighteen gradations, instead of twelve, and connect the points of highest purity, we can see that the curve is parabolic. The fact that the pure, saturated hues, as they appear in the chart of Fig. 58, differ in brilliance, is extremely important. It must be realized that pure saturated yellow is very light, and that there is no such thing as a dark pure yellow. Saturated essential blue is very dark; light blues are pale and dim. Red can emit its considerable vivid power only as a dark color; red lightened to the level of pure yellow loses all radiance. The colorist positively must allow for these facts in his compositions. When a saturated yellow is to produce the main effect, the composition generally must assume a light over-all character, whereas pure saturated red or blue requires a dark over-all expression. The radiant reds in Rembrandt's paintings are so only because

of contrast with yet darker tones. When he wants radiant yellows, he can bring them out in comparatively light groups, where saturated red would be felt as merely dark, without chromatic splendor. Fig. 3 illustrates this principle.

The unlike brilliancies of hues in themselves pose difficult problems for textile designers. Familiarly, any textile design is likely to be produced in four or more different colors or combinations. In the group as a whole, these must be somehow coordinated. A fundamental rule is that corresponding areas of the design should produce the same effect of contrast in each version. If a pure blue occurs in one version, there will not be enough pure hues of similar brilliance to go around among half a dozen other versions; but at least the intervals of brilliance should be alike in all versions. When the blue is replaced by pure orange, the entire color composition must be transposed towards the brilliance level of pure orange. That is, the fabric in which the orange appears must as a whole be lighter than the one with blue. If one attempted to reduce the brilliance of orange to that of the blue, the result would be a dull brown, lacking in radiance.

A serious complication is that the light-dark values of the pure colors vary with the intensity of illumination. Red, orange and yellow look darker in reduced light, while blue and green look lighter. Thus shadings may produce the right effect in full daylight, and yet appear false at twilight. Altarpieces painted for the semiobscurity of churches, therefore, should not be exhibited under skylights in museums or in the glare of artificial light, since the light-dark values of their colors would be falsified.

The plates and exercises in this book are designed to be viewed in full daylight.

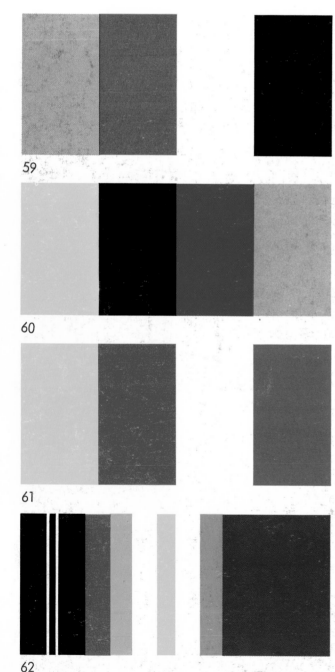

59

60

61

62

Let us notice at this point that to the painter, saturated yellow contains no white and no black; nor is any black or white content seen in pure orange, red, blue, violet, green. When he says that a red contains black or white, he is referring to a shade or tint. For technical purposes, the concept of black or white content may be of use.

We have seen that light-dark polytones may be devised in the so-called achromatic colors – white, gray, black. A light-dark composition may also be developed in tints and shades of any one hue. We have seen that equality of brilliance will relate chromatic colors to grays or to each other. Then we have studied light-dark relationships among the saturated hues. We have found that their tonalities are very different, but that each hue may be lightened towards white or darkened towards black in regular steps.

We shall now have four exercises in light-dark contrasts of black, white, gray and chromatic colors.

Fig. 59 is a tetrad in black, white, gray and one hue. All four differ in brilliance.

Fig. 60 is a tetrad in black, gray and two hues. The black and blue are similarly dark, giving this tetrad two different grades of brilliances.

Fig. 61 is a tetrad in white and three hues, among which red and green are equally dark, and yellow and white about equally bright; two principal tones are present.

Fig. 62 is a hexad in black, white and four hues, exhibiting sharp contrast of proportion. This exercise illustrates the important fact that yellow under certain conditions gives the effect of a darker white, orange that of a darker yellow, and yellowish red that of a darker orange. In the same way, it could be shown that yellow-green can play the part of a darkened, shaded yellow, and green that of a shaded yellow-green. Purple-red and blue can similarly act as tints of violet.

Black, white, the grays, and the color properties just described are the chief elements of plastic modeling.

Fig. 63 represents the development of a light-dark polytone in two dimensions.

A composition painted in light-dark contrast may be constructed of two, three or four principal tones. The painting is then said to have two, three or four chief planes or groupings, which must be well attuned to each other. Each plane may have minor tonal differentiation within itself, but not so much as to blur the distinction between main groupings. An eye for hues of equal brilliance is necessary to the observance of this rule. If tones are not assembled into main groupings or planes, then order, clarity and vigor of composition are sacrificed. An effect of pictorial surface is achieved only with organization in planes.

The necessity of sustaining a flat over-all effect is the painter's chief motive for constructing planes. They serve to frustrate and neutralize any undesired depth effects. This control of perspective results from the equating of tonal values to those of the planes. The planes can usually be grouped into foreground, middle ground and background, but the foreground does not necessarily contain the principal figures; the foreground may be quite vacant, and the main action may take place in the middle ground. Some of our plates may serve as examples. Plates XI and XX have only one plane, Plates V, VII and XIV have two, Plates XV and XXII have three.

The paintings about to be discussed illustrate some of the potentialities of light-dark contrast.

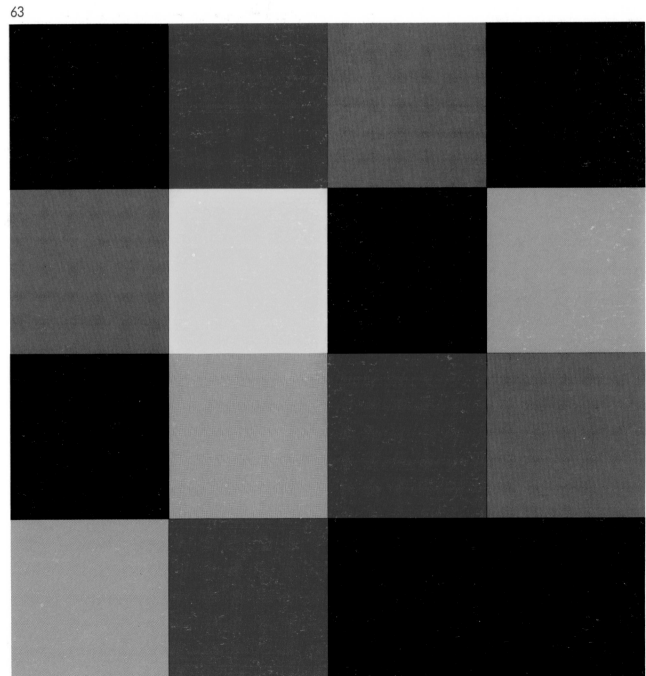

Characteristically, all compositions constructed upon light-dark contrast employ a small number of hues. Another typical feature is the organization of the picture into planes. Because light-dark intonation has great plastic power, modifying surfaces spatially, the painter must plan carefully to control such effects. Organizing the plastically active elements into picture planes is one of the means. This painting is a good example. The picture is constructed in two chief tonal levels. The light tones of the oranges and lemons, the illuminated side of the basket, the light areas of the rose and cup, form one level. The shadows of the fruits and basket and of the plates, cup and rose join themselves to the dark tone of the table and background. The orange blossoms and the highlights of the green leaves belong to the light plane, while their shadow areas belong to the dark plane. The result is a tranquil and pictorial over-all effect, because the tonal differences within each grouping are slight.

Zurbarán's figure paintings also show that he was a profound student of light-dark contrast. His work has a pure and noble manner of great artistic stature.

Rembrandt constructed his paintings in light-dark contrast, for its polytonic possibilities and plastic powers. In this example, the golden helmet is painted in light, warm, yellow-orange tones. The shadows of the embossing are picked out in dark green-gray. The lighted side of the helmet gives an effect of sharp and hard molded texture. The plume, on the other hand, is done in a dull but luminous red, and its dark tone relates the shaded side of the helmet to the background. The man's face as a whole is as dark as the medium tone of the helmet, only the highlights having a brighter value. The face is a wonderful fabric of light and dark, warm and cold, dull and bright hues, vibrant in the shadowy half-darkness. The flesh appears as if painted in depth, pulsating with life. Broad, linear light-dark rhythms solidly suggest the shoulder, while the torso is lost in the dark background. A very important factor in the depth effect of the head is the small highlight on the shoulder. When the beholder half-closes his eyes, he perceives this implicit depth treatment very clearly. Light-dark contrast becomes an arresting medium of expression in this painting.

Rembrandt's "Descent from the Cross" in the Pinakothek at Munich also takes its impact from light-dark effects. In deepest night, the body of Christ is suspended in a drop of liquid light. The white body contrasts with a bluish-white shroud. The yellowish heads of the bystanders are the only warm note. The transition from the light to the dark background is provided by a dull blue-gray to the left of the bright form. The large light area is answered by a small spot of light on the right, the standing man's face. This lends the scene its scale. In the dark tone of the landscape, the attendant figures are illusively indicated.

Plate VII
Pablo Picasso, 1881 - 1973
Guitar on Mantelpiece, 1915.

At the beginning of the twentieth century, a new picture of the world was evolving in science and philosophy. Dimly and subconsciously, young painters felt that new conceptions were bound to emerge in art also.

Cézanne died in 1906, leaving to his successors an estate of challenging ideas. (See analysis of painting "Apples and Oranges," Plate XII.)

Pablo Picasso, Georges Braque and Juan Gris, the three founders of Cubism, carved out a portion of that estate, comprising problems of geometric form. They reduced the multiplicity of shapes to square, triangular and circular elements. Cézanne's polychromatic wealth, which had embraced the entire spectrum, they provisionally limited to black, white, gray, ocher, brown and blue. Light-dark contrast was exploited in all its polytonic resources. Picture surfaces became relief-like configurations, and subject matter was confined to a few homely articles. Musical instruments were favorite subjects because of their refined, functional beauty of form. Painted textures, simulated wood grain and lattice patterns were used as contrasts for linear shapes and unbroken surfaces. Later, actual exemplars of texture such as wood veneers, glass, sheet metal, textiles, wallpaper, newspapers, and single typo-graphical letters of the alphabet were added to the geometrically painted elementary forms. Shapes of objects were detached from their natural organic context and harmonized with abstract geometrical figures. Pictures became non-objective and abstract. Plate VII is such a work by Picasso, painted in 1915.

Objectively, the fireplace and the guitar are merely suggested. The abstract effect of the picture is supported by the deep black and high white. Organization of the several brightnesses into two light-dark planes contributes substantially to the total incorporeal impression. Light areas shine out of the dark general tone of the picture in sharp contrast. The dark red-brown of the background is deepened by black areas, and the brownness is enhanced by the darkness of the blue. A small red-orange area enlivens the dull red-brown. The two bright areas have a mediant in the green and the light textured areas. The black and white stippled area also provides a shading from light to dark. The small white patch at the left and the white spot on the red-orange form a contrast of proportion with the large lighter areas. The tension between the abstract and the objective forms gives the painting its remarkable expression.

64

65

It may seem strange to identify a sensation of temperature with the visual realm of color sensation. However, experiments have demonstrated a difference of five to seven degrees in the subjective feeling of heat or cold between a workroom painted in blue-green and one painted in red-orange. That is, in the blue-green room the occupants felt that 59° F. was cold, whereas in the red-orange room they did not feel cold until the temperature fell to 52-54° F. Objectively, this meant that blue-green slows down the circulation and red-orange stimulates it.

Similar results were obtained in an animal experiment. A racing stable was divided into two sections, the one painted blue, the other red-orange. In the blue section, horses soon quieted down after running, but in the red section they remained hot and restless for some time. It was found that there were no flies in the blue section, and a great many in the red section.

Both experiments illustrate the pertinence of cold-warm contrast to color planning of interiors. The properties of cold and warm colors are essential to color therapeutics in hospitals.

Going back to the color circle, we have seen that yellow is the lightest and violet the darkest hue; that is, these two hues have the strongest light-dark contrast. At right angles to the yellow-violet axis, we have red-orange versus blue-green, the two poles of cold-warm contrast. Red-orange, or minium, is the warmest, and blue-green, or manganese oxide, is the coldest. Generally the colors yellow, yellow-orange, orange, red-orange, red and red-violet are referred to as warm, and yellow-green, green, blue-green, blue, blue-violet and violet as cold, but this classification can be very misleading. Just as the poles white and black represent the lightest and the darkest color, while all grays are light or dark only relatively, according as they are contrasted with lighter or darker tones, so blue-green and red-orange, the cold and warm poles, are always cold and warm respectively, but the hues intermediate between them in the color circle may be either cold or warm according as they are contrasted with warmer or colder tones.

The cold-warm property can be verbalized in a number of other contrary terms:

cold	warm
shadow	sun
transparent	opaque
sedative	stimulant
rare	dense
airy	earthy
far	near
light	heavy
wet	dry

These diverse impressions illustrate the versatile expressive powers of cold-warm contrast. It can be used to produce highly pictorial effects. In landscape, more distant objects always seem colder in color because of the intervening depth of air.

Cold-warm contrast, then, contains elements suggesting nearness and distance. It is an important medium of representation for plastic and perspective effects.

Our exercises on light-dark contrast, especially where equally brilliant colors were adjacent, contained cold-warm contrasts also, as well as contrasts of saturation. However, light-dark contrast was always dominant. When a composition is to be done in the pure style of a particular contrast, all other, incidental contrast must be used with restraint, if at all.

In our exercises on cold-warm contrast, let us eliminate light-dark contrast entirely; that is, all the colors of a composition are to be equally light or dark.

Fig. 64 illustrates cold-warm contrast in its polar antithesis: red-orange/blue-green.

Fig. 65 inverts the proportions by area.

Figs. 66, 67 show the same violet; warm at the top, because the adjacent hues are colder, and cold at the bottom, because the adjacent hues are warmer.

Fig. 68 shows cold-warm modulations in the area of red-orange.

Fig. 69 shows cold-warm modulations in the area of green/blue-green.

These modulations can be executed at any level of tonality, but a medium brilliance is the most effective.

66

67

68

69

The variation of hue should go no further than four successive steps of the 12-hue color circle.

Thus the exercise in red-orange (Fig. 68) uses orange and red-violet, in addition to red-orange and red. The exercise (Fig. 69) in green uses the additional hues yellow-green and blue-green in the same brilliance.

If both poles, the extremes of cold and warm, are to be included, we must form a chromatic scale from blue-green through blue, blue-violet, violet, red-violet and red, to red-orange. This full scale may of course consist of a larger or smaller number of steps. A full chromatic cold-warm scale from blue-green to red-orange by way of yellow is feasible only if all the tones are of the same brilliance as the yellow; otherwise we get light-dark contrast.

These modulations achieve the perfection of their beauty only when light-dark differences are absent.

Whereas Figs. 68 and 69 show chromatic gradations of cold and warm colors, a checkerboard composition heightens the effect by contrast of cold and warm colors (Fig. 70).

When the elementary exercises have been completed, it is interesting to attempt freer forms. For example, representational shapes may be combined with the checkerboard pattern. The colt motif of Fig. 71 is a student's exercise. The active young animal, in a triad of red, red-orange and red-violet, is set in a cold-warm modulation of yellow-green, green, blue-green. The subdivision into squares encourages rich variation within the given key. The painter is compelled to devote thought and decision to each element of area.

This window is one of the earliest examples of French stained glass. It was spared by the fire of 1194, and is now in the south aisle of the cathedral.

When the Abbot of St. Denis, near Paris, first had stained glass windows installed there, in the first half of the twelfth century, he justified his proceeding with the words, "...that the material sense of man may be directed to that which is beyond matter."

These windows were "flashing hieroglyphs," intelligible to all. Their mystic splendor gave the faithful an experience of radiant transcendence. This visual experience was a direct invitation to higher spirituality.

In the Chartres window, the Virgin Mother, in an ice blue dress, is seated on a tall throne, holding the Child, in the exact centerline of the picture. Mary's stiff, straight posture and the central placement allude to a symbolic expression of abstract ideas. This posture conforms to the Early Christian and Byzantine form of representation of the Christ Child as symbolizing rebirth.

The blue of the dress appears against a red-orange ground, lending it a cold, radiant light. The ice blue and red-orange are intense cold-warm contrast.

Today, science tells us that blue stars are young, active suns, whereas red stars are in their declining phase.

This Madonna is the Queen of Heaven, born of the primeval cosmic blue. She shines like a young star, with cold energy, surrounded by the red light of matter. The Child, the incarnate Son of God, is garbed in dark red. The panels of attendant angels were added at a later period. Their design is not consistent in form or color with the central picture. Still, "La Belle Verrière" is a splendid creation and a fine sight to see.

A stained glass window follows the courses of the sun. The angle of the light keeps changing, and the colors are different at each time of day. The translucent glass has the brilliance of precious stones.

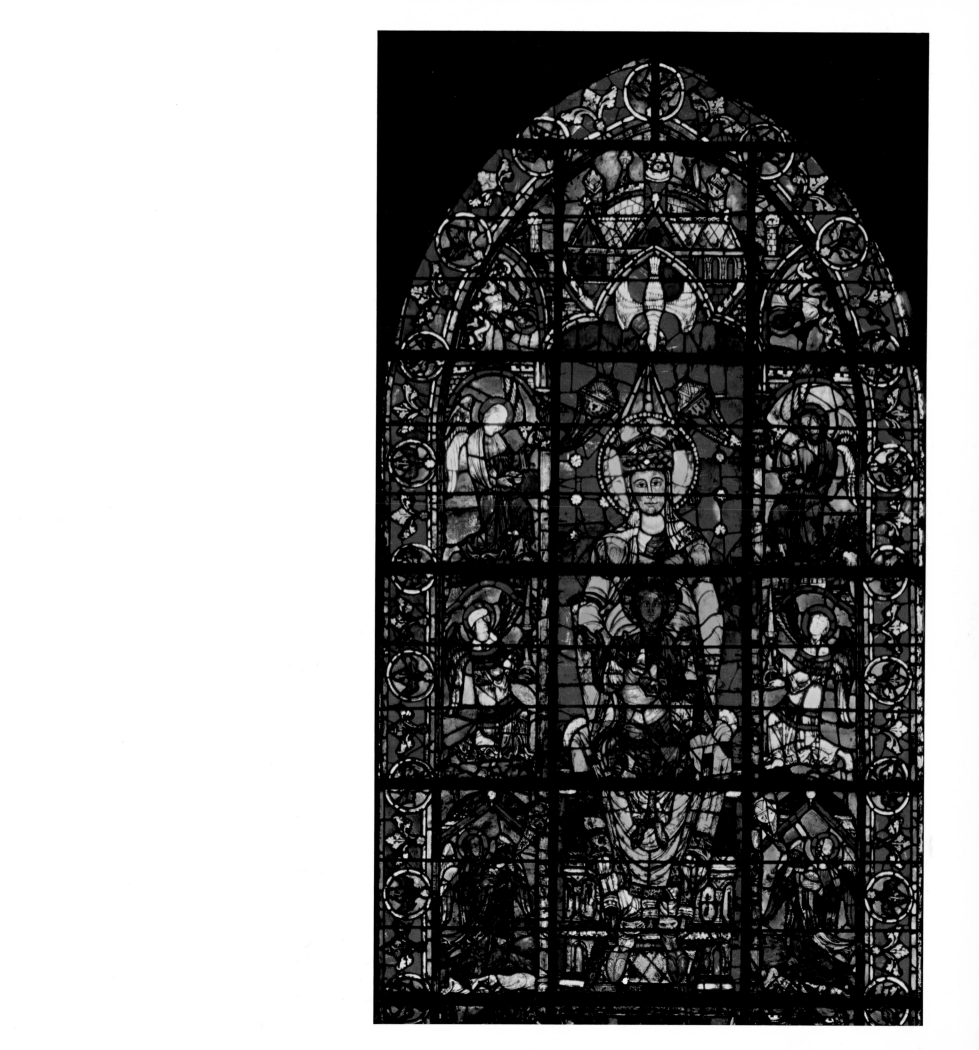

Plate IX
Mathias Grünewald, 1475/80-1528;
Angel Choir,
Isenheim altarpiece; detail.
Colmar, Unterlinden Museum

The Isenheim work was executed for the church of an Anthonin hospital. Among the communicants of this church were many of the sick. To them the paintings were to offer instruction in the meaning of life, its pains and possible joys, as well as comfort and healing to the despondent.

Grünewald chose divergent subjects for the panels. Two subjects – Sebastian and Anthony, and Golgotha and the Lamentation – form a first group. The Annunciation, the Angel Choir, the Virgin and Child, and the Resurrection form the second group. Finally, the two side panels, Anthony and Paul on the left and the Temptation of St. Anthony on the right, form the third group. All of these themes were to be organized into a unified altarpiece. The several groups were to be exhibited to the people according to the ecclesiastical seasons.

In the Isenheim altarpiece as originally composed, the Angel Choir stood between the panels of the Annunciation and the Virgin and Child.

In a Gothic chapel, angels are making music in jubilation at the birth of the Child. Celestial beings discourse supramundane harmony. In this painting, Grünewald proposed to render sound visible.

Of all the seven color contrasts, the cold-warm contrast is the most sonorous. It provides the possibility of representing the music of the spheres in colors. Grünewald chose this contrast for the color design of his Angel Choir, and also for two other parts of the altarpiece – the group of angels attendant upon God the Father in the panel of the Madonna, and the painting of the Resurrection. He employed this color effect in portraying the celestial.

The portion of the Angel Choir reproduced here shows an articulation in three well-defined planes: the bright angel in the foreground, the red-orange group of angels in the middle ground, and the green, violet and blue angels in the background.

The large angel playing the viola da gamba is painted in light cold-warm modulations – warm golden hair, light-and-dark pink garment, light violet to cold blue-green and yellow-green fabric over the foot. The tones appear in the sequence of the color circle. These colors are contrasted with the horizontal red-violet stairsteps.

The heavenly orchestration commences at the point where the angel's hand grasps the bow. Radiating from that point, Grünewald painted a striking concord of violent cold-warm variations. The medium tints of the color circle here shine in their extreme vigor – yellow-green, cold blue, violet, light red, red-orange and yellow. The same hues are repeated in a band of color leading up to the angel in the yellow-green halo. Beside him there is another angel with a pink halo. In the middle ground stands the soloist, clad in hues from cool red to warm orange.

At the right, dark red-brown emits a flame of red, ascending to the red halo of another angel. The warm red and red-orange of this group answers to the groups of cherubim and seraphim in cold green, blue and violet.

Though deep shadows surround the cold-warm chords, yet the cold-warm expression of the picture is distinctly preserved. The angels, pure, lovely, transfigured in colored light, chant their hymn of joy.

Renoir painted this work in 1876, when he was 35. Vendors, seamstresses, clerks and artisans dance on a sunny afternoon in Montmartre; it is an outdoor festival, flooded with light and color.

The entire painting is done in light and dark blue, green, a little yellow and pink. A sweet transparent buoyancy suffuses the atmosphere of the picture. The colors glow diaphanously. Local tones of objects are resolved in the general harmony, translating "hard reality" to a higher plane of spiritualized being. The detail has been chosen because this magical harmony would have been lost in a miniature print of the complete work. Jeanne is the central figure of the painting. Her face is portrayed in modulations of yellowish and pink to light-violet tones, all shading into each other. On the forehead at the right there is a yellow-green, answered by blue-black to dark violet in the border of the hat. The hair is blue-violet, chestnut brown to red-orange, and this note is sustained down to the pink ear, contrasting with the light green at the neckline. The dark cloak boasts a red-violet collar. The yellowish skin tone culminates in the gold of the pendant and ear clip, the pink of the cheeks in the red of the lips. This is intensified by the complementary green tone in the hat, vibrating towards blue and yellow in a lovely cold-warm accord.

The head moves in all but shadowless light. Each hard contour yields to soft transitions. Though shapes are nearly drowned in the sea of light, shape is sensibly there. One is reminded of Cézanne's dictum, "Quand la couleur est à sa richesse, la forme est à sa plénitude." *)

The colors of this painting all have a semblance of reflection, and in their delicate tones they are impalpable and ethereal. One seems to breathe an enchanted air. This effect is owing to cold-warm contrast.

*) When color is in his pride, form is at the full.

72

When Monet began to devote himself to land-scape, he ceased to paint in the studio, and worked out-of-doors. He made intensive studies of seasons, times of day and weather conditions, with their changing light and mood. He meant to portray the shimmer of light in the air and over warm fields, color refractions in cloud and mist, high-lights of flowing, undulant water, and the alter-nation of sunny and shady green in the foliage of trees. He observed that light and shade, and rainbow reflections from all sides, resolved the local colors of objects into elements of cold and warm rather than light and dark variation. In his landscapes, the light-dark contrast emphasized by earlier painting is superseded in importance by cold-warm contrast.

The Impressionists noticed that the cold, trans-parent blue of the sky and atmosphere was every-where in contrast, as a shadow color, with the warm tones of sunlight. The enchantment of Monet's, Pissarro's and Renoir's paintings is achieved by the cunning play of modulations of cold and warm colors.

In the present painting, Monet uses the cold-warm contrast orange/blue-violet. The chromatic modulations of blue-violet/blue-green/yellow-green, contrasting with orange, are woven into a transcendental harmony. The last rays of the setting sun awaken diffuse reflections in the cold, wet fog, obliterating all distinctions of light and dark. Blue-violet tones predominate, expressive of evening.

Plate XII (see pages 76, 77)
Paul Cézanne, 1839 - 1906;
Apples and Oranges.
Paris, Musée Jeu de Paume

Cézanne sought to unite colors and forms into a harmonic organism in later principal works. His insistence on unity occasionally led to formulations in which natural forms and colors are broken up into abstract formal rhythms and color patches. Though seemingly arbitrary, however, Cézanne's analyses never neglected the axioms of ordered composition. He articulated the picture surface in well-proportioned areas, organized polytones in distinct planes, balanced spatial directions with countermovements, and reduced shapes to the clarity of geometrical figures. Whether Cézanne arrived at his proportions by measurement and construction, we do not know. In my opinion, he did measure and construct. When one studies his works closely, it becomes apparent how thoughtful his procedure was. The modulations of colors, rich in relationships; the rhythmic movements of line; the placement of accents – all are well considered.

Cézanne's colors display the whole wealth of their possibilities. Form and color intervals contrast and accord with each other as if in a musical work. "Il joue du grand orgue comme César Franck," was said of him. *)

In the still life "Apples and Oranges," all hues of the color circle are employed, and yet a distinct tetrad of two pairs of complementaries stands out – red/green and orange/blue. The red/green theme appears in the dark form between the light parts of the cloth. The oranges accord with a patch of blue beneath the dish, reverberating in a blue tone of the folds. The four principal colors are distributed

*) He plays full organ, like César Franck.

throughout the surface in diversely modulated patches. A third pair of complementaries, yellow/violet, is subsidiary to the tetrad. Yellow is used as a light accent in the modeling of the apples. Violet enhances the pictorial effect of the composition as a whole. Each hue is used as a pure color, in less saturated tones, and in tints and shades. Cézanne made the less saturated tones by mixing the complementaries red and green, orange and blue, yellow and violet. In this way he obtained mixed tones of great chromatic power, as is particularly manifest in the dark areas. While utilizing all the possible contrasts, he graduated the effects of the contrasting elements. The chief accent of the painting is due to light-dark contrast. A light group consisting of cloth, jug and dish contrasts with the dark portions of the picture. Within these two planes, the colors are varied in a multitude of gradations.

The pictorial color expression of the work results from modulations in cold-warm contrast. On the lighter of the two planes, Cézanne spreads out the entire wealth of cold and warm chromas. For this he uses colors of equal brilliance, taking their chromatic sequence from the color circle. Yellow, green, blue, violet, pink and light orange succeed each other. These cold-warm modulations produce that enchantment of the objective world which Cézanne was striving for.

In the other plane, the colors are not only shaded, but also dulled. The dull tones are placed side-by-side in cold-warm contrast. The use of dilute and pure colors produces effects of saturation contrast.

The modeling of the fruit in light-dark contrast

shows no cold-warm antitheses. The light tones join those of the lighter plane, and the dark tones those of the darker plane.

The outline sketch, Fig. 72, shows salient features of the composition – subdivision of area, spatial directions, contrast of forms and their distribution over the surface. Relationships of accent points and lines are indicated by vertical, horizontal and diagonal axes.

The upward-diverging main lines of the middle picture are interesting. They run contrary to a "normal" perspective, where the lines of a picture converge upon a vanishing point. The two infinite directions are opposed by two pairs of lines intersecng on the upper margin of the picture. Thus the beholder is compelled to concentrate upon the subject.

Cézanne's use of antitheses of form is fundamental. He contrasts round shapes with straight lines and angles, thereby achieving great distinctness in the characterization of forms. The same forms, however, may be connected by other, intermediary forms, and an integrated whole results. The discovery and use of this picture organization is a major achievement of Cézanne.

The distribution of groups and their relation to each other are worked out clearly. In the center of the picture is the big red apple. Groups of fruit, composed in various ways, are arranged on either side and above. The horizontal dish is answered by the vertical jug. The cloth is oriented horizontally and diagonally.

However, the beauty and perfection of the painting does not consist merely in interesting details. The painting is a whole, created with a singleness of purpose.

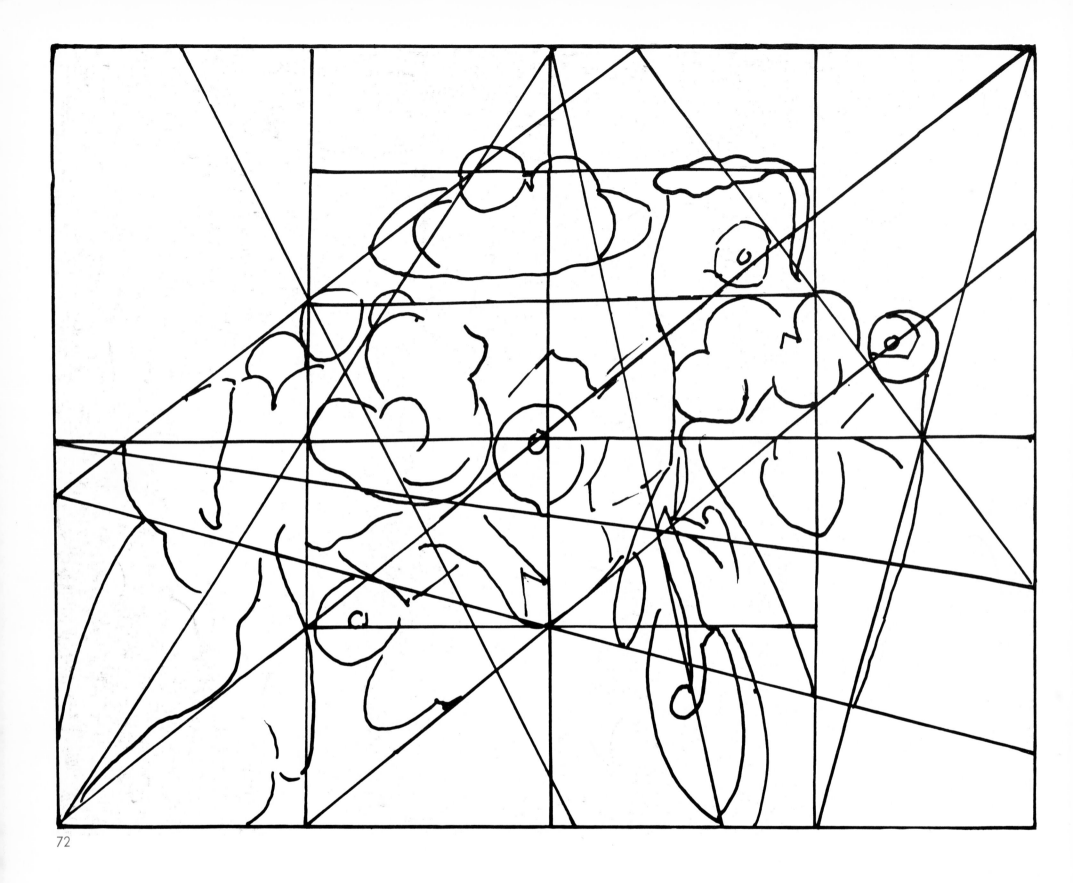

72

Plate XII (see page 75)
Paul Cézanne, 1839 - 1906;
Apples and Oranges.
Paris, Musée Jeu de Paume

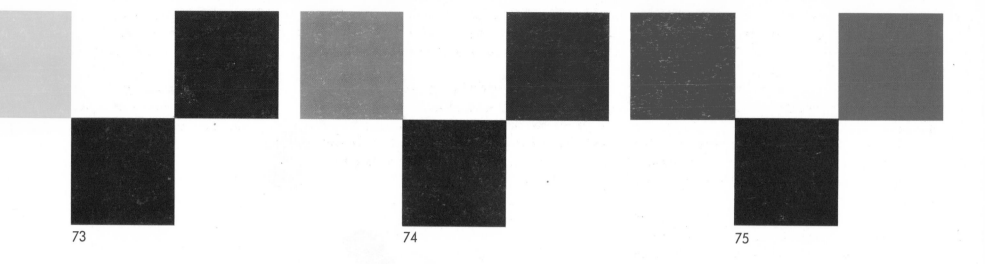

73   74   75

COMPLEMENTARY CONTRAST

We call two colors complementary if their pigments, mixed together, yield a neutral gray-black. Physically, light of two complementary colors, mixed together, will yield white.

Two such colors make a strange pair. They are opposite, they require each other. They incite each other to maximum vividness when adjacent; and they annihilate each other, to gray-black, when mixed – like fire and water.

There is always but one color complementary to a given color. In our color circle, complementaries are diametrically opposite each other.

Examples of complementary pairs are:
>   yellow, violet
>   orange, blue
>   red, green

If we analyze these pairs of complementaries, we find that all three primaries – yellow, red, blue – are always present:

>   yellow, violet = yellow, red + blue
>   orange, blue = blue, yellow + red
>   red, green = red, yellow + blue

Just as the mixture of yellow, red and blue is a gray-black, so the mixture of any two complementaries is gray-black.

We also recall the experiment showing that if one hue of the spectrum is suppressed, all the others mixed together will yield its complementary. For every hue, the sum of all the other colors in the spectrum is the complementary of that hue.

76

77

78

Both the phenomenon of afterimage and the effects of simultaneity illustrate the remarkable physiological fact, as yet unexplained, that the eye requires any given color to be balanced by the complementary, and will spontaneously generate the latter if it is not present. This principle is of great importance in all practical work with color. In the section on concord of colors, we stated that the rule of complementaries is the basis of harmonious design because its observance establishes a precise equilibrium in the eye.

Complementary colors, used in the proper proportions, give the effect of a statically fixed image. Each color stands unmodified in its intensity. Here the agent coincides with the effect. This stabilizing power of complementary colors is especially important in mural painting.

Each complementary pair has its own peculiarities.

Thus, yellow/violet represents not only complementary contrast but also an extreme light-dark contrast.

Red-orange/blue-green is a complementary pair, and at the same time the extreme of cold-warm contrast.

Red and green are complementary, and the two saturated colors have the same brilliance.

Some exercises will help illustrate the nature of complementary contrast.

Figs. 73 - 75 show three complementary pairs and their gray-black mixtures. A little white may be added to the mixture for a more delicate test of the gray. If the mixtures of two colors in all proportions fail to include a neutral gray, it follows that the two colors are not complementary.

Figs. 76 - 78 show three mixture series for as many complementary pairs. These scales are prepared by adding more and more of the complementary to a given color. In the center of each series, we get neutral gray.

Many paintings based on complementary contrast exhibit not only the contrasting complementaries themselves but also their graduated mixtures, as intermediates and compensating tones. Being related to the pure colors, they unite the two into one family. In fact, these mixed tones often occupy more space than the pure colors.

Nature shows such mixed colors very elegantly. They are to be seen in the stems and leaves of a red rosebush before the blossoms appear. The red of the unblown rose mixes with the green of stem and leaf to lovely red-gray and green-gray nuances.

Fig. 79 is a composition in two complementary colors and modulations of their mixed tones.

Of course, two, three or more pairs might be used. The effect is clearest if the complementary color areas touch or are not too far separated.

Two complementary colors can be used to make beautiful chromatic grays. The Old Masters produced such grays by the technique of striping a pure color with coats of the complementary, or by varnishing the first with a thin film of the second. Pointillism produces chromatic grays in still another way. The pure colors are laid side-by-side in tiny dots, and the mixing operation is performed visually in the eye.

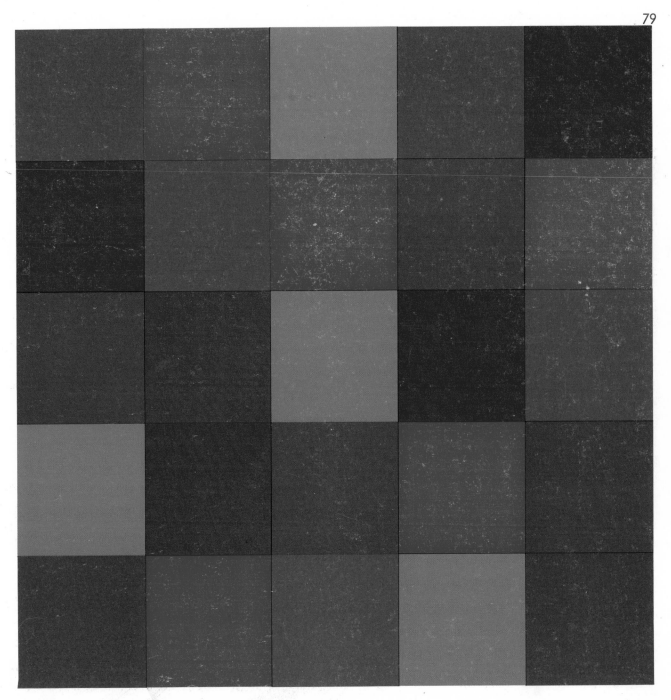

When we compare this Coronation of the Virgin with Charonton's (Plate II), we see a wide discrepancy in conception of the theme. Charonton painted the coronation as a supernal event taking place in heaven. His terrestrial world was small and negligible in relation to the main group of Father, Son and Virgin Mother. This mystical event Van Eyck interprets in an earthly scene where the adoring secular client is represented on the same plane of importance with Mary, about to be crowned by the angel. In realistic style, Van Eyck painted a palatial hall in a lovely setting, and placed his Madonna and Child in this sumptuous worldly milieu. The angel, the representative of the supernatural, is treated as if incidental.

The painting as such is a symphony of contrasts of color, shading, form, proportion and texture. Its color effect is developed from the red of the robe and the green of the lectern cover. These are complementaries. The red is repeated in the angel's wing, in the hem of the blue-green cloth, in the large cap on the small figure on the terrace, and in the background architecture. The colors of the room are mixtures of red and green. Variations on the green of the cloth appear in the angel's blue dress, in the clothing of the figure on the terrace, and in the tints of river, mountains and sky. The suppliant's garb is painted in the hues, darkened and lightened, of the room, repeated in the floor mosaic. The textures of the crown, the border of Mary's robe, the suppliant's costume, the floor, windows, capitals and landscape details lend an expression of great richness.

The multitude of realistically painted minutiae in this picture is characteristic of Van Eyck. He is among those artists who, impressed with the wealth of forms in nature, create in terms of impression.

The Child sits in symbolic benediction on Mary's knee, holding a bejeweled monde of crystal. He is small compared to the seemingly larger-than-life size of the Virgin, evoked by modification of natural human proportions. The red robe is over large, the head very small. Much smaller still is the head of the angel bearing the crown. The patron Chancellor is painted in natural proportions.

This displacement of relative magnitudes is one of the rare qualities of the painting, but characteristic of the painter. Many details of composition display his mastery of proportion.

Plate XIV
Piero della Francesca, 1410/11 - 1492;
Solomon Receiving the Queen of Sheba;
detail of a mural at Arezzo.

King Solomon possessed riches, power and wisdom. Prompted by curiosity and admiration, the Queen of Sheba comes to visit him. He receives her in a great, imposing, richly decorated brocade mantle. This mantle gives an effect of flatness and impassiveness, and reveals a broad descent of blue robe. The cold, negative, unapproachable blue, painted in a hard, rectilinear shape, meets the eyes of the advancing Queen. Her delicately lilac-tinted cloak falls into confused folds as she bows respectfully to Solomon, who, reserved and all but unmoved, gives her his hand. The superior might of the King and the submission of the Queen are joined, in their urbanity and distinction, by the equal brilliances of the royal attire. Solomon's attendants narrowly and expectantly observe the encounter. The Queen's gentlewomen, too, look on with interest. Only the blue-clad lady-in-waiting and the blue-accented gentleman remain coldly aloof from the proceedings.

The chromatic construction of this painting is extraordinary.

The male group at the left is painted in two complementary pairs: orange-brown/blue and purple-red/green.

The dull yellowish gray of Solomon's brocade mantle is in complementary contrast with the Queen's equally light lilac tint. Solomon's yellowish gray suggests his mistrust, likewise expressed in the mask of his countenance. Moreover, his cool and reserved attitude could not be more plainly shown than by the vertical blue stripe of his robe. The Queen's lilac betokens "spiritual infatuation."

The central figures are flanked by the men and women on the left and right. The green dress of a lady answers the red cloak of one of the men. The color arpeggio is unified by the brown-red of the hall.

All of Francesca's paintings have an expression of great calm, an effect not due to coloration alone but also to the static, monumental cast of his forms.

Cézanne stated that he wished to develop Impressionism into something "substantial." His paintings were to be composed with no less logic than those of classical periods. By logical composition he meant organization of the picture into articulate planes, geometrical and rhythmical treatment of natural forms, and a coloration derivable from the relationships and tonalities of the color circle.

Thus on beholding this landscape, one clearly discerns an organization into three horizontal planes. Geometrical and rhythmical treatment of its natural forms is more difficult to discover. But if we overlay a sheet of tracing paper on the print and copy all distinctly accentuated lines and areas, without thought of objective shapes, we are astonished to find rhythms and forms in the tracing that fully reveal the harmony of a Cézanne composition.

The chromatic construction of the painting may be analyzed as follows.

The four colors principally used are set in the three separate planes. In the foreground there is dusky brown-violet. In the middle distance, yellow-green and orange predominate, and in the background, blue. Violet/yellow-green and orange/blue are two complementary pairs, interwoven in complicated "modulations" – Cézanne's own term for his chromatic painting. In the foreground, the brown-violet is modulated in many tones towards brown-red and blue-violet. These tones are moreover varied towards dull and luminous; dull blue tones complete the combination. In the middle distance, where yellow-green and orange dominate, the yellow-green is modulated towards yellow and blue-green, and the orange towards yellow and red-orange. Thus there are chromatic scales from red-orange through yellow to blue-green. Sometimes, light-blue accents appear close beside the complementary orange, as in the orange-yellow spot near the right margin of the plate. The small areas of cold blue contribute much to the rhythmic chord in this plane, and enhance the luminosity of the orange.

The sky and mountain of the background are emphasized in blue. Light blue is modulated towards light green and light violet. The light-violet mountain mass reflects warm orange-browns. In the expanse of sky, luminous light-blue areas alternate with dull green and blue-green.

A glorious chromatic array clothes this canvas, transforming it into a transcendental organism. The device of displacement (see section on composition) is put to powerful use. Blue is displaced into the green-orange and violet planes, green into the blue and violet, violet as a light tone into the blue and as a dark tone into the green. These displacements result in a fabric of color giving the whole picture an expression of unity and open space.

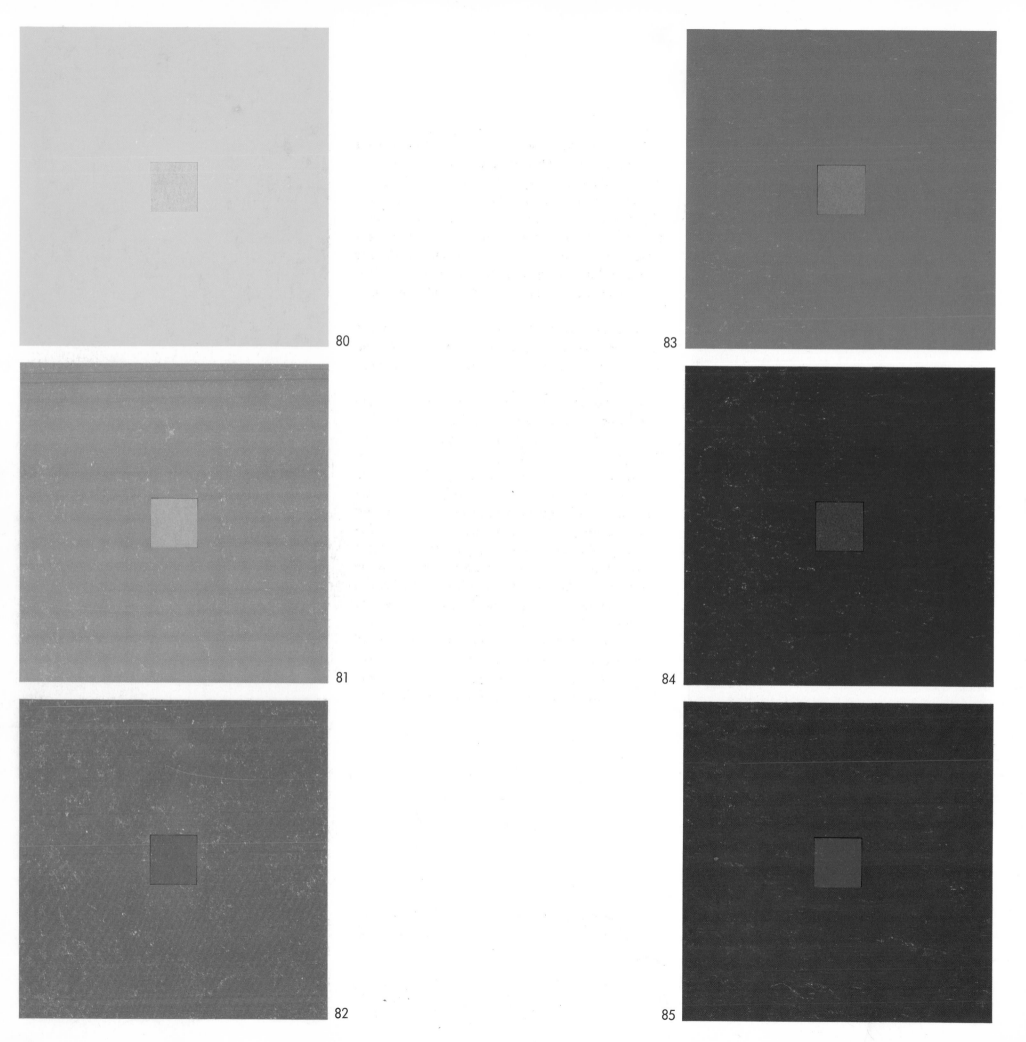

80

83

81

84

82

85

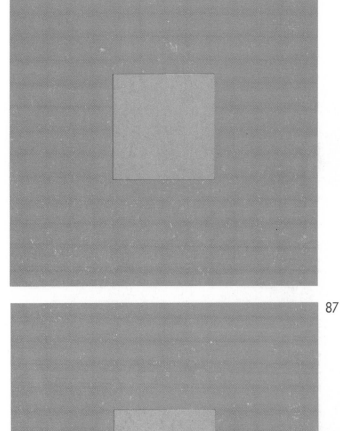

Simultaneous contrast results from the fact that for any given color the eye simultaneously requires the complementary color, and generates it spontaneously if it is not already present. By virtue of this fact, the fundamental principle of color harmony implies the rule of complementaries.

The simultaneously generated complementary occurs as a sensation in the eye of the beholder, and is not objectively present. It cannot be photographed. Simultaneous contrast may with reason be placed on a par with successive contrast.

One may make the following experiment: On a large, strongly colored area, examine a small black square, first laying a sheet of tissue paper on top. If the area is red, the black square will look greenish gray; if green, then reddish; if violet, then yellowish; if yellow, then the black square will look violet-gray. Each hue simultaneously generates its complementary.

Figs. 80 - 85 illustrate this experiment in another form. In each of the six pure colors, I place a small neutral gray square, exactly matching the surrounding color in brilliance. Each of the small squares is tinged, for the eye, with the complementary to the background hue. When gazing at one of the colors, it is best to hide the others and hold the page not too far from the eyes.

Simultaneous effects become more intense, the longer the background is viewed, and the more luminous the color. The effect is intensified if the background is lighted from in front and the example placed slightly below eye level, so that the whole is viewed in obliquely incident light.

The simultaneously appearing color, not being objectively present but generated in the eye, induces a feeling of excitement and lively vibration of ever-changing intensity. Under sustained viewing, the given color seems to lose intensity, as the eye tires, while the sensation of the simultaneous hue grows stronger.

The simultaneous effect occurs not only between a gray and a strong chromatic color, but also between any two colors that are not precisely complementary. Each of the two will tend to shift the other towards its own complement, and generally both will lose some of their intrinsic character

and become tinged with new effects. Under these conditions, colors give an appearance of dynamic activity. Their stability is disturbed, and they are set in changeable oscillation. They lose their objective character and move in an individual field of action of an unreal kind, as if in a new dimension. Color is as if dematerialized. The principle that the agent of a color sensation does not always agree with its effect is fully operative.

Simultaneous effect is of paramount importance to all who are concerned with color. Goethe said that simultaneous contrast determines the aesthetic utility of color.

Figs. 86 - 88 show gray squares in an orange field. Three just perceptibly different grays have been used, as repeated in Fig. 89 below. The gray in the first square is bluish, intensifying the simultaneous blue effect (Fig. 86). The gray in the second square is neutral, and a normal simultaneous effect is obtained (Fig. 87). In the third orange square, the gray looks neutral (Fig. 88). The reason for this difference in the effects of the three grays is that a little blue has been mixed with the first gray, and this cooperates with the simultaneous effect; the second gray is neutral, and shows the simultaneous effect alone; while the third gray contains an admixture of orange just sufficient to cancel the simultaneous effect, and therefore shows no simultaneous modification. This experiment clearly shows how the exciting effect of simultane-

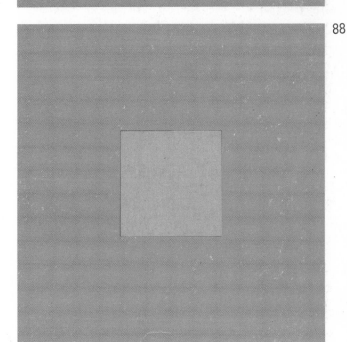

90

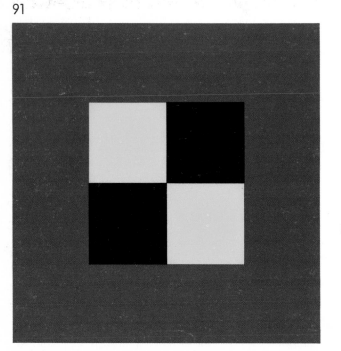

91

ous contrast can be amplified or suppressed by suitable devices.

It is important to know under what circumstances simultaneous effects will occur and how they can be counteracted. There are many problems in color that preclude solutions using simultaneous contrast. Some years ago, the manager of a weaving mill called my attention, in desperation, to some hundreds of meters of costly tie silk that would not sell because a black stripe on a red ground looked, not black, but green. This effect was so pronounced that customers insisted that the yarn was green. If brownish black yarn had been used, the simultaneous effect would have been neutralized, and heavy losses avoided.

In addition to the means of preventing simultaneous effect as illustrated in Fig. 88, there is another possibility; the susceptible hues may be used in unlike brilliance. Once a light-dark contrast is present, simultaneous influences are diminished.

It is always advisable to juxtapose the hues to be employed in a composition, using a preliminary sketch to check color effects, before proceeding to execution.

Some exercises will further clarify the foregoing.

In Fig. 90, we have two black squares on a violet ground. They show a simultaneous greenish tinge.

In Fig. 91, there are two black and two yellow squares on the violet ground. The black shows hardly any simultaneous influence towards green, because the yellow complementary to the violet is present.

92

93

In Fig. 92, two greenish black and two red-orange squares are set on red-violet. Red-orange demands blue-green, and red-violet demands yellow-green; hence the greenish black is quite strongly viridescent, green being between yellow-green and blue-green in the color circle. The red-orange and blue-green likewise undergo strong simultaneous excitation.

Fig. 93 shows red-violet and red-orange on green. Red-violet calls for blue-green, and green calls for red, the color between red-orange and red-violet. The green has the power to make both the red-violet and the red-orange more reddish, and both show an irritated simultaneous rubescence. This is a true simultaneous effect in pure colors.

Analogous experiments can of course be carried out with all the other hues.

Fig. 94 shows that the primary colors yellow and red look static on blue, with no simultaneous modification of each other. If, as in Fig. 95, the blue background is modified towards blue-green, simultaneity sets in; the yellow and red are simultaneously excited on blue-green.

Simultaneous effects occur among pure colors when a complementary hue is replaced by its right- or left-hand neighbor in the 12-hue color circle. For violet, for example, in opposition to yellow, we substitute red-violet or blue-violet. Effects of simultaneous contrast can be intensified with the aid of contrast of extension; compare Figs. 104 and 105.

95

94

Plate XVI
Satan and the Locusts,
from the Apocalypse de Saint Sever, 11th century.
Paris, Bibliothèque Nationale

The illuminations in this work date from the eleventh century. "Satan and the Locusts" exerts an uncommonly expressive power. Both choice of hues and division into areas are strikingly original in composition.

The picture is constructed in two planes. One of these, forming the background, is divided into eight equal horizontal rectangles, presenting two pairs of colors – red-orange/green and brown-violet/yellow. Each color is arranged in two rectangles, diagonally. The other plane consists of the figures – Satan, the locusts, and human beings. For them, two more pairs of colors are used – blue/orange and white/black. Thus the picture comprises a combination of eight colors. The two pairs red-orange/green and brown-violet/yellow are not exactly complementary pairs. Each generates simultaneous contrast, and therefore the effect of the colors is vibrant and discordant, as the theme requires. The locusts and the human figures on the red-orange/green background are done in blue and brown-violet, whereas on the brown-violet/yellow background they appear in blue and green. The blue of the men and of the locusts gives an effect of confusion; to stalk their prey, the Devil and the locusts take on a piety that is not theirs. White and black lend some abstractness to the representation.

The expression of the colors and shapes is enhanced by the gestures and postures of the locusts urged on by their master. The painting as a whole suggests savage cruelty and treachery. The ever-changing orientation of human and arthropod figures portrays the aggressiveness of the forces of evil and the helpless despair of the victims.

Expressional works of art often have a repellent effect, wholly at variance with the notion of classical beauty. Grünewald's "Temptation of St. Anthony" and "Crucifixion" pertain to the same expressive genre. Such works evoke strong emotion in the beholder, who must feel the destructive power of creative activity.

Plate XVII
El Greco, 1541 - 1614;
Stripping of Christ.
Munich, Pinakothek

El Greco began to paint in Venice, as a pupil of Titian. However, the gloomy, passionate style of Tintoretto and the attenuated pictorial differentiation of Veronese influenced him more than Titian's subtle polytonality.

In his paintings, El Greco intensified the passionate motion of Tintoretto's figures to ecstatic vision, and transformed Veronese's restrained color into free, expressive harmonies. Physical perspective and anatomy, with El Greco, become expressive, pictorial. Cézanne was to claim and cultivate this legacy.

El Greco looked to action and color for an expression of his experience. He developed objectively correct color concords for each subject, leaving the treatment of form to subjective bias.

This painting shows El Greco's characteristic qualities. The subject is one of the ugliest and most repulsive incidents of the Passion. El Greco contrasts the kingly greatness and presence of Christ with the rude mob of men-at-arms. Christ stands apart, robed in purple, in the center of the picture, assaulted by the soldier in black-green. Beside the heavenly King, stands the knight in gray-blue armor of proof, a symbol of warlike temporal dominion.

The steel harness of this hypocritical, passive, indifferent looker-on reflects the purple of the robe, mingling with the gray-blue to dramatic blue-violet.

In the left foreground stand the two Marys, their eyes averted. The one is in dull gray-yellow, the other in dull dark-blue. At the right, a workman in a brash greenish yellow vest stoops over a timber with his auger. He is working on the cross. His motion, the foreshortened body and sulphur yellow vest connote a casual falseness. His white shirt suggests detachment from the actual scene.

In the middle field, there jostles an amorphous mass of excited soldiery. The gray-blue of the man in armor is repeated horizontally in the background. The many nervously scattered lights in the general blue-gray create a hard, metallically cold atmosphere. The component colors purple, greenish yellow, gray-yellow and blue-gray irritate each other into a discordant, desperate simultaneous contrast of great sharpness. This simultaneous effect occurs because the colors are not precisely complementary, and interfere. El Greco has expressed a feeling of oppression in this way. He has sacrificed "beauty of color" to veracity of mood.

Plate XVIII
Vincent van Gogh, 1853 - 1890;
Café at Evening.
Otterloo, Rijksmuseum Kröller-Müller

From Impressionism and Neo-Impressionism, Van Gogh developed an expressionism of rhythmic line and strong color. He transformed the statics of Neo-Impressionism, with their foundations in the science of color, into dynamics governed by subjective experience. The "pointille" of color is enlarged by Van Gogh and used to texture the color area. He uses texture as a means of rhythmicizing and intensifying colors. Van Gogh's pictures are drawn as if by a cursive movement, and his coloration is determined by expressive considerations. Most of his paintings are shatteringly expressive. The colors are not, in our sense, harmonious.

This example shows a brightly lit sidewalk café by night. The region flooded with warm light is painted flat in yellow and orange. These bright colors contrast with dark buildings and the starry blue-violet night sky. Van Gogh's paved street becomes an area textured with dots and dashes of yellow, orange, light blue and black. The blue-violet of the sky is repeated in the doorway at the left. Occasional spots of orange in the blue-black housefronts suggest lighted windows. A few figures are lost in the depth of the dark street. Belated customers are sitting towards one end. Empty chairs and tables, people homeward bound, and the few lighted windows, lend an expression of solitude and desertion. Other paintings of Van Gogh's, such as "The Sower," "The Yellow Armchair," "Seated Old Man," similarly reflect his personal isolation.

In the present painting, Van Gogh relates the loftiness of the nocturnal sky to the smallness of human individuals and to their imprisonment in self-chosen surroundings. Artificial light is in antithesis to the eternal light of the stars. Thus every particle of the picture is permeated with the humor of the painter's melancholy.

The principal color, yellow, together with the orange of the café, forms a simultaneous contrast to the blue-violet of the sky. Violet would have been complementary to yellow, and blue to orange. But instead of violet and blue, Van Gogh chose a blue-violet that sets both the yellow and the orange in vibration. This effect is intensified by unbalanced area distribution. The glaring yellow and orange would require a much larger expanse of blue-violet for harmonious equilibrium. The yellow-green of the walls and the dark green of the tree generate another simultaneous contrast with the interspersed spots and streaks of red. This asymmetry of composition lends expressionistic intensity to the coloring of the picture.

96 · 97 · 98

CONTRAST OF SATURATION

Saturation, or quality, relates to the degree of purity of a color. Contrast of saturation is the contrast between pure, intense colors and dull, diluted colors. The prismatic hues produced by dispersion of white light are colors of maximum saturation or intensity of hue.

We have colors of maximum saturation among pigments also. We recall the curve pointed out in Fig. 58, connecting pigmentary colors of highest purity and intensity.

Colors may be diluted in four different ways, with very different results.

1) A pure color may be diluted with white. This renders its character somewhat colder. Carmine assumes a bluish cast as it is mixed with white, and becomes sharply altered in character. Yellow is cooled by white; the character of blue is hardly changed. Violet is extremely sensitive to white. Whereas saturated dark violet has something menacing about it, violet lightened with white — lilac — has an agreeable and quietly cheerful effect.

2) A color may be diluted with black.
This admixture deprives yellow of its brilliant character, turning it into something sickly or insidiously poisonous. Its splendor is gone.

Géricault's picture "Les Aliénés" is in black-yellow, and has an overwhelming expression of mental derangement.

Violet is enhanced by black in its "inherent" gloom, fading as it were into night.

By admixture of black, carmine acquires a timbre in the direction of violet.

Vermilion diluted with black gives a kind of burnt, red-brown pigment.

Blue is eclipsed by black. It will suffer only a few degrees of dilution before its light is extinguished.

Green admits of far more modulation than violet or blue, and has many possible alterations.

Quite in general, black deprives colors of their quality of light. It alienates them from light, and sooner or later deadens them.

3) A saturated color can be diluted by mixing it with white and black, or in other words with gray. As soon as I mix gray with a saturated color, I get tones which may be of equal, greater or less brightness, but in any case less intense than the corresponding pure color. Admixture of gray renders colors more or less dull and neutral.

Delacroix hated gray in a painting, and avoided it as much as possible. Mixed grays are easily neutralized by simultaneous contrast effects.

4) Pure colors may be diluted by admixture of the corresponding complementary colors. If I add yellow to violet, I get tones intermediate between the light yellow and the dark violet. Green and red are not much different in tonality, but when mixed they descend into gray-black. The various

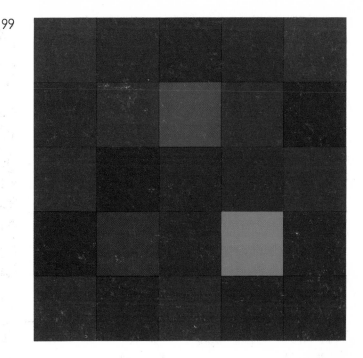

mixtures of two complementary colors lightened with white produce rare tints.

When a mixture contains all three primaries, the resulting hue assumes a dim, diluted character. Depending on the proportions, it will appear yellowish, reddish or bluish gray or black. All degrees of dilution can be obtained with the three primaries. The same applies to the three secondaries, or to any other combination provided only that yellow, red and blue are all present in the total mixture.

The effect of "dull-vivid" contrast is relative. A color may appear vivid beside a dull tone, and dull beside a more vivid tone.

Basic exercises in contrast of saturation can be performed on a checkerboard of twenty-five squares. We place a pure color in the center, and a neutral gray of the same brilliance in each of the four corners. We then mix gray with the pure color step-by-step, obtaining four more or less diluted intermediates. To comprehend contrast of saturation, we must eliminate light-dark contrast; hence the brilliances of all squares must be the same. The exercises of Figs. 96 - 98 show the delicate character of this contrast in its chromatic modulations. Similar exercises can be done by placing the complementary of the central color in the corner squares, instead of gray. The effect will then be more lively.

Fig. 99 shows three luminous colors of equal brilliance along with neutral gray. Here we see how gray neutralizes strong colors into a quiet effect.

If we wish to express pure contrast of saturation in a composition, without any other contrast, then the dull color must be mixed from the same hue as the intense one; that is, intense red must contrast with dull red, and intense blue with dull blue.

Otherwise, the pure contrast would be drowned out by other contrasts, such as cold-warm contrast, impairing the quiet and restful effect.

Dull tones, most especially grays, live by virtue of the vivid ones surrounding them. This may be observed by dividing an area checkerboard-fashion and placing a neutral gray in every other square, with vivid colors of the same brilliance as the gray in the remaining squares. The gray will be seen to take on vividness; while the surrounding chromatic colors appear reduced and comparatively weakened.

Plate XIX
Georges de la Tour, d. 1659;
Newborn Babe.
Musée de Rennes

De la Tour was a master of high reputation in his own lifetime. He worked at Lunéville, where he died in 1659. Thereafter his paintings fell into oblivion until the Cubists and Expressionists rediscovered them. His subjects are plain and workaday, but abruptly remote and difficult of access. He had a predilection for nocturnal scenes with marked chiaroscuro. Tintoretto and Caravaccio had anticipated this style. Tintoretto sometimes modeled his motifs in wax or clay, and studied the resulting plastic sketches by candlelight to discover the correct distribution of light. De la Tour, in his endeavor to represent lighting effects as convincingly as possible, went so far as to include the source of illumination, the lighted candle, in some of his paintings. The result is a realistic distinctness, not at all in the manner of Rembrandt, who solved the problem of light in a rather more abstract way.

The painting "Newborn Babe" represents a young mother and her sleeping infant. Another woman, facing her, is holding a lighted candle.

The principle of composition here is no less pure than in the paintings of Francesca. Definite posture of figures is as important to orderly composition as definite accentuation of horizontal, vertical and diagonal directions in space. De la Tour has the mother in full face, the other woman and the child in profile. Postures generally correspond to direction of attention, and both women are looking at the child. The hand shading the light of the candle is likewise offering a benediction and assisting the concentration of gaze upon the infant. Everything near the tiny head is plastically accented, while more distant forms are less distinctly depicted. De la Tour's way of passing tints and shades across the figures achieves a dematerialization of natural forms. Thus a shade joins the child into one pictorial element with the background. The same shade inhibits perspective effect from knee to head of the mother, thereby preserving unity of the picture plane. The white of the second woman's dress passes in delicate darkening transitions to her head and into the obscurity of the background.

The coloration of De la Tour's paintings is pronouncedly subjective. He used the same colors almost invariably – red, black and white – and the contrasts of brilliance and saturation, constructing his compositions in light and dark, vivid and dull colors. The use of contrast of saturation transforms fiery red into quiet warmth. Although light-dark contrasts are often violent, the general effect of De la Tour's work is restrained. Its expression is more given to meditation than to spectacle.

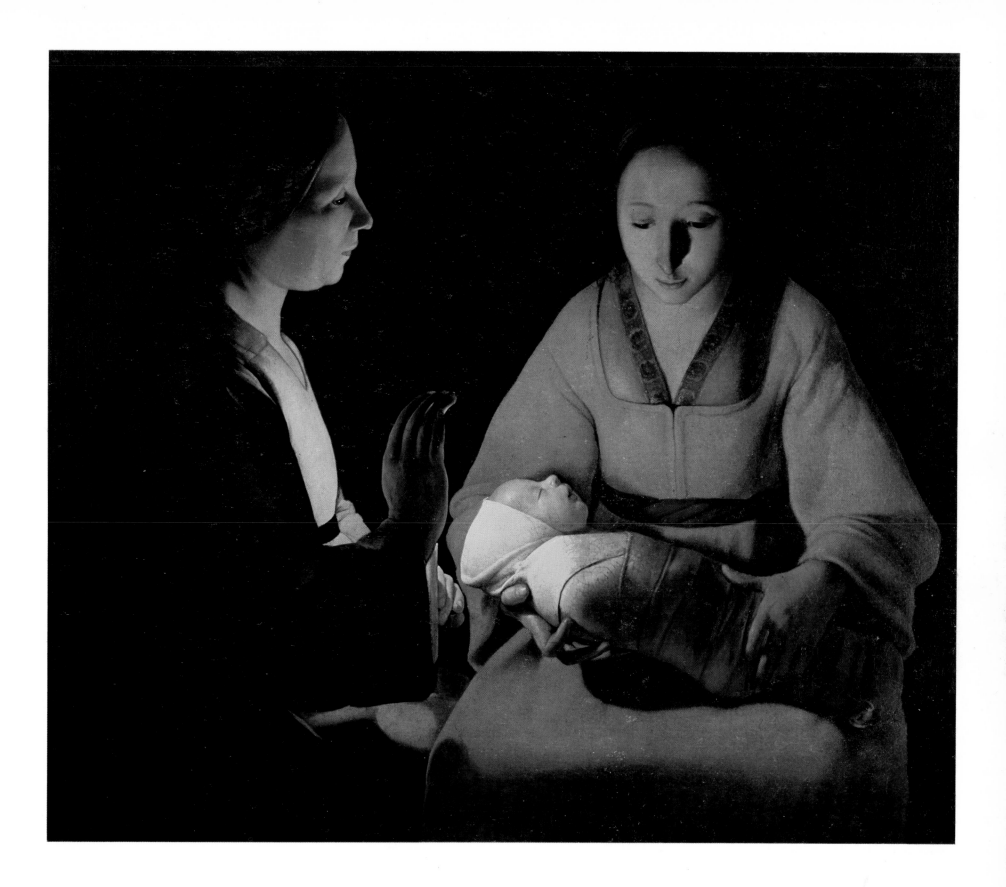

Matisse was one of the Paris group of painters called "Les Fauves". They continued Gauguin's experiments with large color areas. Matisse's paintings are constructed in a great variety of color contrasts. When he places black or white next to pure colors, they too become chromatic elements. Over many years of activity, Matisse increasingly negated local color and modeling in light and shade. His paintings became more and more flat and abstract. "Plus c'est plat, plus c'est de l'art," was his motto. *)

Matisse painted this piece in 1916. It is very quiet as a whole, and all colors are of equal brilliance except for the rather narrow black striping of the piano and the light figure in the background.

The dull gray-green principal tone underlies the large swathe of clear green at the left, the equally brilliant stripe of blue and its nearly complementary light red-orange. The intense green against the gray-green, which is dull but of the same brilliance, is pure saturation contrast. On the piano there is a cloth of pink, complementary to the green, with a small yellow-green candlestick upon it. This last has an important function. Whereas the pianist merges with the general atmosphere, the candlestick provides the center of tension among the green, pink and black. Chromatically, it is an augmentation of the green into yellow-green.

The arabesques of the music rack are echoed in the rhythmic grille of the window. The light figure on the high stool is no doubt the reflected image of a listener, beheld or imagined by the boy performer while playing.

*) The more flat, the more art.

Plate XXI
Paul Klee, 1879 - 1940;
Magic Fish.
Philadelphia, Museum of Art

Klee's work generally presents an uncommon breadth in the use of color resources. He practiced all the possibilities of color effect, and cannot be reduced to any specific character of coloration or expression. His was an austere, cheerfully somber melody of all the chromatic entities beneath, above and upon the earth. Klee loved colors and treated them accordingly.

In the Magic Fish painting before us, two main contrasts are at work, the light-dark contrasts in the blue-white, pink and orange tones, and saturation contrast in the red and dark blue shades. The background is blue-black night, out of which pure colors luminesce here and there, like tropical fish darting into the light.

It is a quarter to twelve by the clock suspended over the center of the picture. Shortly before midnight, the slender, magical blue fish rises in the pond. He floats, all but invisible, horizontally to the right of the clock. When the clock strikes twelve, he will dart forth to claim his domain. All the fishes float in horizontal attitude, awaiting the magic blue advent. Below, near the hourglass vase of five flowers, there stands a Janus-faced figure, hearkening and beckoning in uncertain expectancy. In the lower left-hand corner, another figure peers obliquely upward; for in the egg cup, a great round red egg glows. Above, one of the goldfish radiates the light lilac of fascination – being held by the gaze of the blue fish, or so one might interpret the puffs of blue above and below the captivated lover. The full moon shines motionless overhead, and warm red curtains entice into the piscine bower – at a quarter to twelve of a blue-black night.

This painting bristles with mischievous confabulation.

100

101

102

CONTRAST OF EXTENSION

Contrast of extension involves the relative areas of two or more color patches. It is the contrast between much and little, or great and small.

Colors may be assembled in areas of any size. But we should inquire what quantitative proportion between two or more colors may be said to be in balance, with no one of the colors used more prominently than another.

Two factors determine the force of a pure color, its brilliance and its extent. To estimate brilliance or light value, we must compare the pure colors on a neutral-gray background of medium brilliance. We find that the intensities or light values of the several hues are different.

Goethe set up simple numerical ratios for these values, best suited to our purpose. They are approximate, but who would demand precise data when commercial pigments sold under the same name can vary so widely? Ultimately, vision must decide. Furthermore, the color areas in a painting are often fragmentary and complicated in shape, and it would be difficult to reduce them to simple numerical proportions. The eye is trustworthy enough, provided it be properly sensitized.

Goethe's light values are as follows:

yellow : orange : red : violet : blue : green
   9   :   8   : 6 :   3   : 4   :   6

The proportionalities for complementary pairs are:

yellow : violet $= 9 : 3 = 3 : 1 = \frac{3}{4} : \frac{1}{4}$
orange : blue $\ = 8 : 4 = 2 : 1 = \frac{2}{3} : \frac{1}{3}$
   red : green $= 6 : 6 = 1 : 1 = \frac{1}{2} : \frac{1}{2}$

In converting these values to harmonious areas, I must take the reciprocals of the light values; that is, yellow, being three times as strong, must occupy only one-third as much area as its complementary violet.

As Figs. 100 - 102 illustrate, we obtain the following harmonious relative areas for the complementaries:

yellow : violet $= \frac{1}{4} : \frac{3}{4}$
orange : blue $\ = \frac{1}{3} : \frac{2}{3}$
   red : green $= \frac{1}{2} : \frac{1}{2}$

The harmonious areas for the primary and secondary colors are therefore as follows:

yellow : orange : red : violet : blue : green
   3   :   4   : 6 :   9   : 8   :   6
Or:

yellow : orange $= 3 : 4$
yellow : red $\quad = 3 : 6$
yellow : violet $\ = 3 : 9$
yellow : blue $\quad = 3 : 8$
yellow : red : blue $= 3 : 6 : 8$
orange : violet : green $= 4 : 9 : 6$

− and so forth; all the other colors are to be related to each other similarly.

Fig. 103 shows the primary and secondary color circle of harmonious extension. This is constructed as follows:

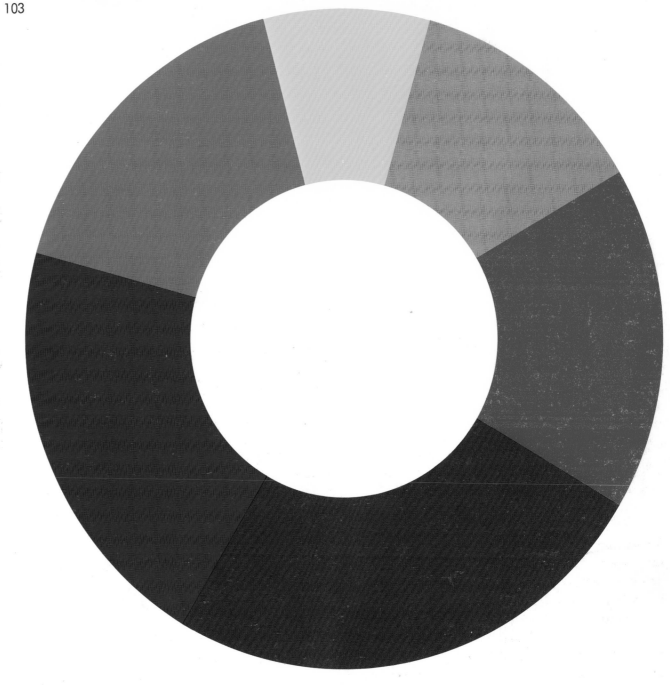

First, a whole circle is divided into three equal parts and each third is in turn divided in the proportions for two complementary colors.

One third of the circle is divided for yellow : violet :: 1/4 : 3/4,

Another third is divided for orange : blue :: 1/3 : 2/3, and

The last third is divided for red : green :: 1/2 : 1/2.

When all these arcs have been found, another equal circle is drawn, and the sectors are transferred in the sequence of the prismatic color circle, namely yellow, orange, red, violet, blue, green.

Harmonic areas yield static, quiet effects. Contrast of extension is neutralized when the harmonious proportions are used.

The ratios here stated are valid only when all the hues appear in their maximum purity. If these are altered, the equilibrium areas also change. The two factors of light value and extent of area turn out to be most intimately related.

If other than harmonious proportions are used in a color composition, thus allowing one color to dominate, then the effect obtained is expressive. What proportions are to be chosen in an expressive composition depends on subject matter, artistic sense and personal taste.

What effect is obtained when contrast of extension is very pronounced? In Fig. 104, blue is represented in such small quantity as to be just noticeable. In Fig. 105, red holds a minority.

As orange is present in very large quantity compared to blue in Fig. 104, it simultaneously generates the full vividness of its complementary blue in the eye. It was stated in the section on simultaneous contrast that the eye demands the complement to a given hue. It is not yet known why this is so. Perhaps we are ruled by some universal will to compensation or counterassertion. Contrast of extension owes its special effect to a similar tendency. The minority color, in distress, as it were, reacts defensively to seem relatively more vivid than if it were present in a harmonious amount. A similar law of compensation is seen to operate in biology. In plants or animals, under adverse conditions of life, there is a mobilization of powers of resistance, expressing itself in heightened performance, given the opportunity. If a color present in minute amount is given opportunity, by protracted contemplation, to assert itself in the eye, it is found to become increasingly concentrated and provocative.

105

In Fig. 105, yellow-green is comparatively extensive, but since red is not exactly complementary to yellow-green, the effect of contrast of extension is supplemented by that of simultaneous contrast. The red is not only intensified, but also distinctly modified in its redness. The use of two mutually intensified contrasts can produce very live and strange color expressions.

A special property of contrast of extension is here exemplified; it is capable of modifying and intensifying the effect of any other contrast. Mention was made of proportion under the heading of light-dark contrast. Contrast of extension is, properly speaking, a contrast of proportion. In light-dark composition, if a small bright spot contrasts with a large area of darkness, this antithesis may lend the picture an enlarged and deepened significance.

Plate VI, "Man in Golden Helmet," may serve as an example. The small bright patch on the shoulder is necessary for proportion of the head. Contrast of hue behaves similarly. In Mondrian's Composition (Plate IV), the small yellow area determines the proper scale. Attention to the color areas in composition is at least as important as the actual choice of colors. Any color composition should be evolved from the relationships of elements of area to each other.

Color areas should take their form, extent and outline from chroma and intensity of color, and not be predetermined by delineation.

Observance of this rule is particularly important to the proper determination of color extensions. The correct sizes of color areas are not to be laid out by means of outline, since the proportions are governed by the chromatic forces evolving out of hue, saturation, brilliance, and contrast effects.

A yellow area that is to hold its place among light tints must be of a different size than an area of the same yellow against dark shades. The tints call for a large yellow area; among shades, a small yellow area is enough to allow the brilliance of the hue to operate. Proportions of all color areas should be similarly derived from their relative potentials. In the Brueghel painting discussed on the next page, the red-orange of the sleeve, despite the smallness of the area, is able to assert itself as a strong accent in the picture.

The work of the Flemish master is wholly different in expression from the contemporaneous painting of Italy. Renaissance opulence and idealism yield place in Bruegel to realistic representations of his rustic surroundings and to genre illustration. He painted no idealized individual figures, but peasant assemblages, larger and smaller clusters of people. Rather than Madonnas, he portrayed profane folk types, with their crimes and passions, labors and festivals. His scenes are populous village squares and broad, detailed landscapes. These settings are just as important to him as the cast of characters.

In the "The Fall of Icarus" the persons take their places on the expanse of magnificent landscape as on a stage. In the foreground, a plowman follows the plow, a shepherd minds his grazing flock, and a fisherman perches at the water's edge. Sailboats run before the wind; in the distance lies a town, and mountains rise. Islands break the surface of the sea, and, at the horizon, the sun appears. Another day has begun, and all are at their accustomed tasks. No one notices Icarus tumbling into the sea, and none is mindful of his fate. Brueghel's realistic opinion of the hero is quite plain.

The color is local, and subservient to exposition. It is without expressive signification. The small amount of red-orange in the sleeve and collar of the plowman is in contrast of extension with the blue-green, green and brown shadings of the picture as a whole. Bruegel used another kind of contrast of proportion, great-small contrast, in coordinating the three different bulks of the big farmer, smaller shepherd and small angler. Then there are the islet, reef and rock in the sea, or the sailing vessel, fisherman, and drowning Icarus.

The spatial problem is attacked in a special way. Diagonals lead the eye into the depths of the picture. One diagonal extends from the angler through the flock of sheep to the base of the abrupt, light-colored rock. This is answered by a countermovement from the rock through the town to the sun, the center of vision on the horizon. The same point is the target of a diagonal from the plow to the plowman's head and continuing to the rock and the small ships. Still another diagonal runs from Icarus through the wind-filled sail to the sun. The diagonals contrast with the horizon, the horizontal from the town to the island at sea, and the horizontal from the promontory at the right through the sail, rock and dark tree at the left. The static effect of the picture is reinforced by verticals, one at the left from horse through tree trunks to high rock, one at the right from fisherman through Icarus to mast and distant peak.

The concentration and solitude of each human being in the great landscape lends the painting an expression of fateful community between man and nature.

106

To acquaint ourselves still further with the color kingdom, let us try some exercises in systematic mixing. According to sensitivity and technique, we may choose few or many intermediate degrees.

Any color may be mixed with black, white or gray, and any color may be mixed with any chromatic color. The innumerable possible mixtures constitute the copious variety of this universe.

1. Mixture Bands

We place any two colors at the ends of a strip, and prepare graduated mixtures of the two. Depending on the two colors with which we begin, we shall obtain some scale of mixed tones. These may be varied into tints or shades (Figs. 76 - 78).

2. Mixture triangles

We divide each side of an equilateral triangle into three equal parts, and join the points of division by lines parallel to the sides of the triangle. This makes nine small triangles. In the corner triangles, we place yellow, red, and blue, and we mix yellow with red, red with blue, and blue with yellow, for the triangles midway between the corners. In each of the remaining triangles, we place the mixture of the three colors adjoining it (Fig. 106). The same thing is done beginning with red, blue and green (Fig. 107).

3. Mixture squares

Figs. 108, 109 show mixture squares. This array is very instructive when, as starting points, we place white, black, and a pair of complementaries in the four corners (Fig. 108). Or we may take two pairs of complementaries (Fig. 109); or again, any four colors may be placed in the corners. In doing this exercise, we begin by painting in the mixtures between the given colors along the edges, and then the progressions along the diagonals. Lastly, we interpolate the missing tones chromatically.

The tones of a mixture triangle or square form a complete family, all interrelated.

Anyone wishing to explore further the possibilities of color mixing should try mixing each hue with each of the others. Rule off a large square into

107

13 by 13 small squares. The first space at the upper left is kept white. The remaining squares of the top row are filled in with the twelve hues of the color circle from yellow through yellow-orange to yellow-green. The remaining squares of the left-hand column are filled in with the same hues in complementary sequence, from violet through blue-violet and blue to red-violet. The second row is completed by mixing each hue of the first row with violet. In the third row, each hue of the first row is mixed with blue-violet. When each hue of the left-hand column has been mixed with each hue of the top row, then the large square will show a diagonal of grays from upper left to lower right, where the complementaries meet.

El Greco, Rembrandt, Cézanne and other masters produced remarkable mixtures by over-laying transparent pigments. Seurat and the Neo-Impressionists instead placed pure hues side-by-side, to form additive mixtures in the eye of the beholder.

When the student has completed a number of exercises in mixing colors, he may proceed to reproduce given tones as accurately as possible by mixing. Models may be taken from nature, works of art, or any other source. I think the value of such practice lies in improved perception of colors and verification of that perception by precise repro-duction. Just as in the most delicate industrial processes, measurement and calculation ultimately break down, and the right result can be obtained only through the skill of the specially endowed craftsman, so the artistically decisive mixtures and compositions of colors can be perfected only through color sense.

Generally speaking, sensitivity to color is biased in the same way as subjective taste. Persons of a blue subjective timbre will perceive numerous variations of blue, but possibly very few of red. It is therefore worth while to carry the exercises through the whole domain of colors. In this way we become more just in our evaluation of all colors.

Besides the pigmentary method of color mixing thus far discussed, there is also the method of visual mixing. This consists in juxtaposing the pure colors to be mixed in small areas or dots, and then viewing the resulting dotted surface, or pointillé, from some distance. In the eye, the dots are mixed into a unitary color sensation. The advantage of this additive kind of mixing is that the resulting tones are less diluted and more vibrant.

The same breakdown of color areas into elemen-tary dots is employed in color printing. The eye unites the dots into continuous areas. When the reproduction is viewed through a magnifier, the minute dots of color can be seen individually. In ordinary four-color printing, the many different shadings are produced by combinations or mixtures of four standardized colors, yellow, blue-green, bluish red and black. Obviously these four compo-nents and their mixtures will not always yield the utmost fidelity of reproduction. When extremely high quality of rendition is to be achieved, seven or more color plates are used.

Another everyday example of subjective color mixing is to be found in weaving. Differently colored warp and woof threads combine, according to the weave, into a more or less integrated field. A familiar pattern is that of the Scottish plaids. Where a set of colored warp threads intersects a group of weft threads of the same hue, squares of pure vivid color occur. Where the intersecting threads are of unlike hue, the warp and weft colors are mixed; the area actually consists of differently colored dots, but it looks homogeneous at some distance. The original tartan patterns, woven in fine wool, were the heraldic property of particular clans. The proportions and coloring of genuine tartans are models of textile design to the present day.

108

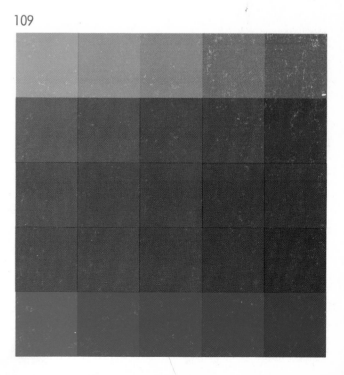

109

Seurat tried to organize seemingly arbitrary aspects of the Impressionist movement in painting into a well-constructed and objectively supported whole.

He would have the almost random color patches of a Monet assembled into regular color groupings based on physical laws. The luminosity of colors was to be intensified by analyzing mixed tones into their elementary components, and then applying these pure colors to the canvas in dots. The eye of the beholder was left to produce the mixed tone. The rule of complementaries played a large part, because the ultimate effect of the painting was to be a harmonious gray.

Seurat also returned to a cultivation of form, and his paintings are architectonic in arrangement. He was keenly interested in problems of light and shade. His pictures are constructed in light-dark planes and patches. In our example, the foreground is a horizontally oriented dark expanse in which luminous colors and light and dark patches deepen and relieve the green.

In the light middle plane, the pale green is accented with complementary red and the cold light-blue of the river. The background of the picture is formed by dark foliage, terminating the scene horizontally at the top. The dark group of figures at the right bridges the middle ground, joining foreground and background by its vertical span. The individual color areas are resolved into restlessly vibrating modulations of contrasting tones.

The painting is broken down into dots of contrasting color, and despite some strong hues the total effect is very quiet. Typical color areas for study are the group in the left foreground, the dress of the lady standing at the right, and the light and dark greens. None of these areas are painted in homogeneously mixed colors; each consists of many distinguishable notes, meeting as smooth textures only in the eye of the observer.

COLOR SPHERE AND COLOR STAR

Having given an account of the potential effects of colors in their seven contrasts, I shall attempt to provide a clear and complete map of the world of color. In Fig. 37, we developed a 12-hue color circle from the three primaries yellow, red, blue. However, this circular array is not adequate for a complete classification. Instead of a circle, we shall need a sphere, the solid adopted by Philipp Otto Runge as the most convenient for plotting the characteristic and manifold properties of the color universe. The sphere is the elementary shape of universal symmetry. It serves to visualize the rule of complementaries, illustrates all fundamental relationships among colors, and between chromatic colors and black and white. If we imagine the color sphere to be a transparent body, each point within which corresponds to a particular value, then all conceivable colors have a place.

Each point on the sphere can be located by its meridian and parallel. For an adequate color classification, we require only six parallels and 12 meridians.

On the surface of the sphere, we draw six equally spaced parallel circles, forming seven zones. Perpendicular to these zones, we draw 12 meridians from pole to pole. On the equatorial zone, in the 12 uniform quadrilaterals obtained, we place the pure colors of our 12-hue color circle. The two polar zones are occupied by white at the top and black at the bottom. In the two zones between white and the equatorial zone, we inter-polate two evenly spaced tints of each hue. Between the equatorial zone and the black zone, we interpolate two evenly spaced shades of each hue. Since the 12 pure colors have unequal brilliances, the degrees towards white and black must be adjusted for each color separately. The pure color yellow is very light, and its two tints are therefore close together, whereas its two degrees of shade are far apart. Violet is the darkest of the pure colors, and its tints are widely spaced, whereas its shades are close together. Each of the 12 hues must be lightened and darkened beginning from its normal brilliance, so that we have two zones of tints and two zones of shades of the 12 hues, in each of which zones the tonality varies. Thus the yellow in the zone of first tints is lighter than the violet in that zone. The zones are not belts of uniform brilliance of the twelve hues.

Since we cannot reproduce the color sphere in three dimensions here, we project the spherical surface on a plane. If we view the color sphere from above, we see the white zone in the center, then the two zones of tints, and then half of the equatorial zone of pure colors. Viewing the sphere from below, we have the black zone in the center, then the two zones of shades, and then the other half of the equatorial zone.

In order to see the entire surface of the sphere at once, we may imagine the darker hemisphere to be slit at the meridians and developed in the same plane as the lighter hemisphere. The result is the 12-pointed star of Fig. 110. White is in the center. Reading outward, we have the zones of tints, the zone of the pure hues, and the two zones of shades, with black at the extreme points of the star.

111a

111b

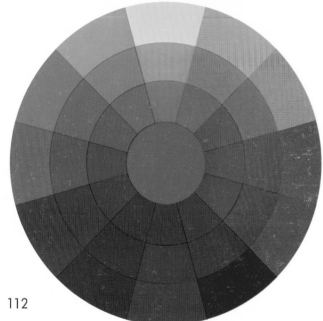

112

113

Fig. 111a shows an equatorial view of the color sphere. The equatorial zone contains the pure colors, lightened with white in two degrees of brilliance towards the white pole. Towards the black pole, the pure colors are shaded with black in two degrees of darkness. In Fig. 111b the other side of the sphere is represented in the same manner, thus covering the entire surface.

In order to find out what is going on inside the sphere, we must take sections.

Fig. 112 shows a horizontal section of the color sphere at the equator. We note the neutral gray region in the center, and the ring of pure hues on the outside. The two strata between the pure colors and the gray are the mixed tones of the corresponding complementary colors.

Such a cross section might of course be taken through any of the brilliance zones of the sphere.

In the center of the sphere, the series of grays extends along the axis between the white and black poles. Our diagram, as has been mentioned, has only seven degrees of brilliance. The fourth degree must therefore correspond to the middle gray between white and black, and that middle gray is the center of the sphere.

The same gray is obtained by mixing any two complementaries. Therefore if we take two opposite hues of the equatorial zone, we get a complete set of gradations, as we did in Figs. 76 - 78 and in the section on complementary colors. In the horizontal cross sections of the color sphere, we confine ourselves to five intermediates between opposite extremes, the central mixture being neutral gray.

Fig. 113 shows a vertical section of the color sphere, taken in the red-orange/blue-green sector. Looking at the equatorial zone of this section, we find blue-green at the left and red-orange at the right in maximum saturation. Towards the axis, we find two mixed degrees of each of the two saturated hues. The resulting seven equatorial chromas are tinted towards white and shaded towards black. Such vertical sections may be passed through any pair of complementary colors and the black and white poles. The several tonalities of any level of lightness or darkness should in this case be equal, and match the gray of that level.

By painting all the horizontal and vertical sections of the sphere in this manner, we complete our color catalogue. Horizontal sections contain the degrees of saturation of the hues, and vertical sections contain the tints and shades of a given pair of complementaries, pure and diluted. Such exercises heighten color sensitivity to light-dark values and to degrees of saturation.

The following, then, are the colors we can construct by means of the color sphere:

1) The pure prismatic hues, located on the equator of the spherical surface;

2) All mixtures of the prismatic hues with white and black, in the brilliance zones of the surface;

3) The mixtures of each complementary pair, as exhibited in a horizontal section;

4) The mixtures of any complementary pair, tinted and shaded towards white and black, as represented in the corresponding vertical section.

Suppose we have a double-pointed needle universally pivoted at the center of the color sphere. Let one point of the needle be directed at any spot on the sphere; then the other point will indicate the symmetrical spot, or complementary color value. If one end points at the second tint of red, namely pink, then the other end will point at the second shade of the complementary green. If we point one end at the second shade of orange, namely brown, then the other will point at the second tint of blue. Thus not only the opposite hues but also all their degrees of brilliance are in complementary relation to each other.

Fig. 114 shows the five principal paths of transition between two contrasting colors. If we begin with a complementary pair, say orange and blue-green, and try to find intermediates between the two, we first locate the two colors on the color sphere. Orange, which lies on the equator, may be modified towards blue along the equator by way of red and violet or else by way of yellow and green. These are the two horizontal paths. Alternatively, the same orange can be connected with blue along the meridian, either by way of light orange, white and light blue, or else by way of dark orange, black and dark blue. These are the two vertical paths.

By following the diameter of the color sphere from orange to blue, the two complementaries may be joined by way of gray and other mixtures of orange and blue, in the order of orange-gray, gray and blue-gray. This is the diagonal path.

These five principal paths are the shortest and simplest lines of transition between the two contrasting hues.

If it be imagined that this systematic classification of colors and contrasts banishes all difficulties, I should add that the kingdom of colors has within it multidimensional possibilities only partly to be reduced to simple order. Each individual color is a universe in itself. We must therefore content ourselves with an exposition of fundamentals.

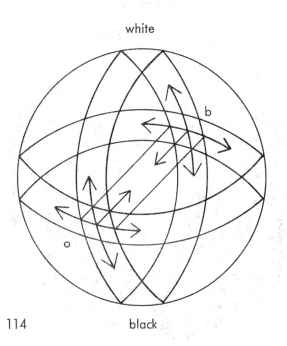

white

b

o

114   black

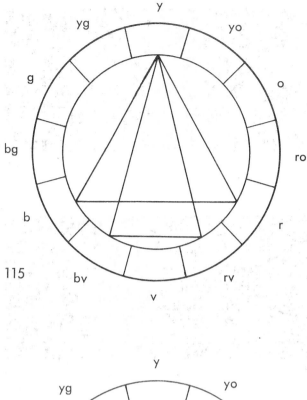

115

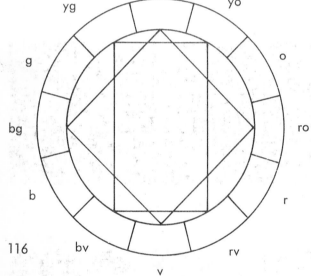

116

white

black

117

By color harmony I mean the craft of developing themes from systematic color relationships capable of serving as a basis for composition. Since it would be impossible to catalogue all combinations here, let us confine ourselves to developing some of the harmonic relationships.

Color chords may be formed of two, three, four or more tones. We shall refer to such chords as dyads, triads, tetrads etc.

1. Dyads

In the 12-hue color circle, two diametrically opposed colors are complementary. They form a harmonious dyad. Red/green, blue/orange, yellow/violet are such dyads. If I use the color sphere, I can get an indefinite number of harmonious dyads. The only requirement is that the two tones be symmetrical with respect to the center of the sphere. Thus if I take a tint of red, the corresponding green must be shaded in the same degree as the red is lightened.

2. Triads

If three hues are selected from the color circle so that their positions form an equilateral triangle, those hues form a harmonious triad.

Yellow/red/blue is the clearest and most powerful of such triads; see Fig. 118. I should be inclined to call it the fundamental triad. The secondary colors, orange/violet/green, form another distinctive triad.

Yellow-orange/red-violet/blue-green, or red-orange/blue-violet/yellow-green, are other triads whose arrangement in the color circle is an equilateral triangle.

If one color in the complementary dyad yellow/violet is replaced by its two neighbors, thus associating yellow with blue-violet and red-violet, or violet with yellow-green and yellow-orange, the resulting triads are likewise harmonious in

character. Their geometrical figure is an isosceles triangle, as Fig. 115 shows. These equilateral and isosceles triangles may also be thought of as inscribed in the color sphere. They may be rotated at will. Provided the point of intersection of the bisectors of their sides lies at the center of the sphere, the three colors related by their vertices make a harmonious triad. Two limiting cases occur when one vertex of the triangle is at white or black. If we use an equilateral triangle with one vertex at white, the other two vertices will point to the first shades of a pair of complementary hues. Then we get such a triad as white/dark blue-green/dark orange. Similarly, for black we get light blue and light orange.

These limiting cases illustrate how light-dark contrast will assume prominence when white or black is used.

3. Tetrads

If we choose two pairs of complementaries in the color circle whose connecting diameters are perpendicular to each other, we obtain a square, as in Fig. 116. The three tetrads of this kind in the 12-hue circle are:

yellow/violet/red-orange/blue-green
yellow-orange/blue-violet/red/green
orange/blue/red-violet/yellow-green

More tetrads are obtained with a rectangle containing two complementary pairs:
yellow-green / red-violet / yellow-orange / blue-violet
yellow/violet/orange/blue

A third geometrical figure for harmonious tetrads is the trapezoid. Two hues may be adjacent, and two opposing ones found to the right and left of their complements. The resulting chords tend to simultaneous modification, but they are harmonious; for when mixed, they produce gray-black.

By inscribing the polygons shown in Fig. 116 in a color sphere and rotating them, a very large number of further themes could be derived.

118

119

120

4. Hexads

Hexads may be derived in two different ways.

A hexagon, rather than a square or triangle, may be inscribed in the color circle. Three pairs of complementary colors are then obtained as a harmonious hexad. There are two such hexads in the 12-hue circle:

yellow / violet / orange / blue / red / green
yellow-orange / blue-violet / red-orange / blue-green / red-violet / yellow-green

This hexagon may be rotated in the color sphere. The resulting tints and shades yield interesting color combinations.

The other way to construct a hexad is to adjoin white and black to four pure colors. We place a square in the equatorial plane of the color sphere, obtaining a tetrad of two complementary pairs. Then each vertex of the square is joined to white above and black below, as shown in Fig. 117. The result is a regular octahedron.

Any tetrad obtainable in the equatorial plane may thus be expanded into a hexad by inclusion of white and black.

A rectangle may be used instead of a square; and an equatorial triangle combined with white and black yields pentads, such as yellow/red/blue/black/white or orange/violet/green/black/white, etc.

Now that these elements of a color harmony have been suggested, it should again be emphasized that the choice of a chord and its modulation as the basis of a composition cannot be arbitrary. All procedures are governed by the subject matter, presented representationally or abstractly. The choice of a theme and its execution are a must, not a capricious will or a superficial maybe. Each color and each group of colors is an individual of unique kind, living and growing according to its immanent law.

The idea of color harmony is to discover the strongest effects by correct choice of antitheses.

Fig. 118 shows the fundamental chord as defined above. In terms of this example, we shall show how the most diverse variations can be derived from a geometrically constructed theme.

One variation consists in surrounding yellow by blue or red, or red by yellow or blue, or blue by yellow or red.

Fig. 119 shows the hues of the fundamental chord combined with their weaker tones.

Fig. 120 shows an example of transposition of the fundamental chord, which is a contrast of hue, into a contrast of saturation, by dilution of individual tones.

Fig. 121 shows tints and shades of the hues of the fundamental chord, forming a harmony in light-dark contrast.

Fig. 122 shows all three hues lightened to the same brilliance, while the pure colors are scattered in small quantities. This is a harmony in contrast of extension. Such variations might be continued indefinitely. If one color predominates quantitatively, timbres of expressive value result.

By going on to replace a pure color of the chord by its immediate neighbors in the color circle, thus substituting yellow-green and yellow-orange for yellow, or red-orange and red-violet for red, or blue-green and blue-violet for blue, the triad is expanded into a tetrad, greatly enlarging the wealth of variations.

These suggestions are intended to show that a theory of harmony does not tend to fetter the imagination, but on the contrary provides a guide to discovery of new and different means of color expression.

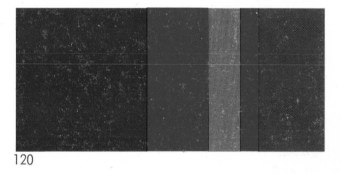

121

122

FORM AND COLOR

In the section on theory of color expression, I shall attempt to describe the expressive potentialities of colors. However, shapes also have their "ethico-aesthetic," expressive values.

In a pictorial work, these expressive qualities of form and color should be synchronized; that is, form and color expressions should support each other.

As is true of the three primary colors, red, yellow and blue, the three fundamental shapes – square, triangle and circle – may be assigned distinct expressive values.

The square, whose essence is two horizontal and two vertical intersecting lines of equal length, symbolizes matter, gravity and sharp limitation. The Egyptian hieroglyph for "field" is a square. A marked tension is felt when the straight sides and right angles of the square are drawn and experienced as motion. All shapes characterized by horizontals and verticals may be assimilated to square form, including the cross, the rectangle, the Greek key, and their derivatives.

The square corresponds to red, the color of matter. The weight and opacity of red agree with the static and grave shape of the square.

The triangle owes its nature to three intersecting diagonals. Its acute angles produce an effect of pugnacity and aggression. The triangle assimilates all shapes of diagonal character, such as the rhombus, trapezoid, zig-zag, and their derivatives. It is the symbol of thought, and among colors its weightless character is matched by lucid yellow.

A circle is the locus of a point moving at constant distance from a given point in a plane. In contradistinction to the sharp, tense sensation of motion produced by the square, the circle generates a feeling of relaxation and smooth motion. It is the symbol of the spirit, moving undivided within itself. The ancient Chinese used circular elements to build their temples, while the palace of the temporal sovereign was constructed in quadrangular manner. The astrological symbol for the sun is a circle with a dot in the center.

The circle comprehends all shapes of flexuous, cyclic character, as the ellipse, oval, wave, parabola, and their derivatives. The incessantly moving circle corresponds among colors to transparent blue.

To summarize, the square is resting matter; the radiating triangle is thought, and the circle is spirit in eternal motion. If we look for shapes to match the secondary colors, we find the trapezoid for orange, a spherical triangle for green, and an ellipse for violet; Fig. 123.

Coordination of given colors with corresponding shapes involves a parallelism. Where colors and shapes agree in their expression, their effects are additive. A picture whose expression is determined chiefly by color should develop its forms from color, while a picture stressing form should have a

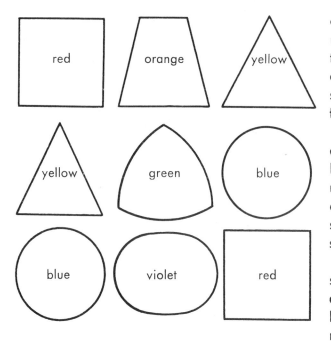

123

coloration derived from its form. The Cubists were most particularly interested in form and reduced their colors in number accordingly. Expressionists and Futurists used both form and color as expressive media; Impressionists and Tachistes dissolved form in favor of color.

What has been said of subjective color holds also of form. Each individual's constitution endows him with certain traits. Graphology inquires into the relationship between subjective form in handwriting and the personality of the writer, but only certain subjective forms can manifest themselves in lineal script.

The Chinese calligraphers admired works of subjective originality, but a scroll was most esteemed if at once original and harmoniously balanced. Brush-and-ink painting was similarly regarded. Liang K'ai and other masters went a step further. They placed no value on originality and personal style; they sought the absolute in art, and attempted to give each subject a formal expression of general validity. Liang K'ai's works differ so in line and tone that it is not easy to identify the artist. Subjectivity of form is submerged in his paintings in the interest of a higher, objective fidelity.

In European painting, Matthias Grünewald aspired to the same objectivity, in form and color. Konrad Witz and El Greco were largely objective as to color, but subjective as to form. De la Tour's work is subjective in form and color alike. Van Gogh's paintings, also, are subjective in both draftsmanship and coloration.

Painting is rich in objective categories. They lie in spatial direction, distribution of mass, free selection of forms and areas with their tonalities and textures.

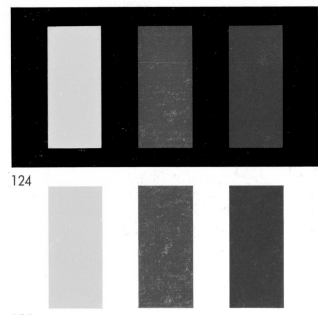

124

125

126

The spatial effect of a color may be a resultant of several components. Forces acting in the direction of depth are present in the color itself. They may manifest themselves in light-dark, cold-warm, saturation or extension. In addition, a spatial effect may be produced by diagonals and overlappings.

When the six hues, yellow, orange, red, violet, blue and green, are juxtaposed, without intervals, on a black ground, the light yellow plainly appears to advance, while violet lurks in the depth of the black background. All the other hues are intermediate between yellow and violet. A white background will alter the depth effect. Violet seems to advance from the white ground which holds back the yellow with its kindred brilliance. These observations show how the background color is as essential to depth effect as the applied color. Here we have another instance of the relativity of color effects, discussed in the sections on agent and effect, simultaneous contrast, and color expression.

Back in 1915, studies of depth effect in colors led me to the conclusion that the six fundamental hues on a black ground conform to the ratio of the Golden Section in their gradation of depth.

To divide a line segment according to the Golden Section, let the shorter part bear the same proportion to the longer as the longer bears to the whole length. If the Golden Section of a segment AB is at C, then AC (the shorter part) is to CB as CB is to AB. AC is called the "minor" and CB the "major."

When orange is interposed in the depth interval from yellow to red, the depth intervals from yellow to orange and from orange to red are as minor to major. Similarly, the intervals from yellow to red-orange and from red-orange to blue are as minor

to major. Yellow-to-red and red-to-violet are in the same proportion. Yellow-to-green and green-to-blue are as major to minor.

In Fig. 124, yellow, red-orange and blue appear on black; in Fig. 125, the same colors appear on white. The depth movement on black is as follows: yellow is strongly advancing, red-orange less so, and blue is nearly as deep as black. On white the effect is reversed; blue is thrust forward from the white ground, red-orange less so, and yellow only slightly so. The depth intervals from yellow to red-orange and from red-orange to blue are as major to minor. The fact that this impression does not depend on the sequence of the colors can be verified by rotating the illustration through 90° or 180°. True, our habit of reading and writing from left to right may cause a difference in scale, but the proportion of the intervals is unaltered.

Any light tones on a black ground will advance according to their degree of brilliance. On a white ground, the effect is reversed; light tones are held to the plane of the background, and shades approaching black are thrust forward in corresponding degree.

Among cold and warm tones of equal brilliance, the warm will advance and the cold retreat. If light-dark contrast is also present, the forces in the direction of depth will be added or subtracted or will cancel out. When equally brilliant blue-green and red-orange are seen against black, the blue-green retreats and the red-orange advances. If the red-orange is lightened somewhat, it advances still further. If the blue-green is lightened, it advances to the same level as the red-orange; if lightened sufficiently, it advances further and the red-orange recedes.

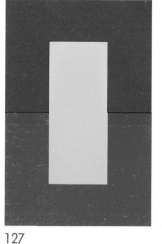

127

128

129

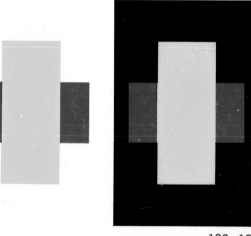

130 · 131

132 · 133

134 · 135

The depth effects of saturation contrast are as follows: a pure color advances relative to a duller one of equal brilliance, but if light-dark or cold-warm contrast is also present, the depth relationship shifts accordingly.

Extension is another factor of depth effect. When a large red area bears a small yellow patch, the red acts as a background and the yellow advances. As the yellow is extended and encroaches on the red, a point is reached where the yellow becomes dominant; it expands into a background and thrusts the red forward.

Even if we were to analyze all possible depth effects of color combinations, it would give us no guarantee of spatial equilibrium in a color composition. The individual discrimination and intention of the artist must govern.

To illustrate the spatial potency of diagonals, the hues, yellow, red-orange and blue, have been arrayed in two diagonal directions on a black background in Fig. 126. We see that the movement in depth from yellow to blue has been accentuated. Below, it runs from near left to far right; above, from near right to far left. The two contrary depth movements intersect in red-orange. The same exercise can be performed in reverse on a white background.

Other depth effects are illustrated in Figs. 127 - 135.

Fig. 127 shows yellow over red-orange and blue, with blue at the top and red at the bottom. Yellow advances sharply, red and blue recede, blue more so than red. Because the yellow overlaps the midline, the plastic effect is strengthened.

Fig. 128 shows the same arrangement except that blue is at the bottom and red at the top. This time, the red thrusts the blue forward, itself remaining in depth. We thus see that location at the top or bottom of the field may affect the apparent depth of colors.

Fig. 129 shows the three colors in equal brilliance. This greatly attenuates their depth effect.

Figs. 130 and 131 show the colors blue and yellow on white and on black. The blue shape overlaps the yellow, and is more prominent in both illustrations. The blue is joined to the black background in Fig. 131 and the depth effect is weaker than in Fig. 130. In Figs. 132 and 133, the shapes are the same as before, but now yellow overlaps blue. It fuses to the white background, weakening the plastic effect, but on black the natural depth properties of yellow and blue are fully realized.

In Figs. 134 and 135, finally, the same forms appear on white and black without overlapping. On white, blue looks like a hole in the field and yellow advances somewhat. On black, blue floats just ahead of the background and yellow advances prominently.

These few experiments can only hint at the problems of pictorial depth illusion. To assess colors as factors of depth, one must train one's vision in these comparisons. "Ne faites pas des fenêtres!" said Corot – no holes in the picture; or let us say, painters must be careful of depth effects.

A very common solution to the spatial problem has been to organize all shapes and colors of a picture into two, three or more planes. As many as five planes are used in the landscapes of Claude Lorrain. Two planes give the flattest and the most pictorial expression. A typical example of this solution is Plate V, Zurbarán's painting "Lemons, Oranges and Rose."

The study of color impression properly begins with color effects in nature. That is, we investigate the impressions made by colored objects on our sense of vision.

One day in 1922, shortly after Kandinsky's appointment to the faculty of the government Bauhaus at Weimar, Gropius, Kandinsky, Klee and I were talking when Kandinsky turned to Klee and myself and asked, "What subjects are you teaching?" Klee said he was lecturing on problems of form, and I explained about my introductory course. Kandinsky rejoined dryly. "Good, then I'll teach nature study!" We nodded, and nothing more was said about the curriculum. For a number of years after this, Kandinsky gave instruction in analytical studies from nature.

It is symptomatic of a lack of orientation in art schools today that the necessity of nature study can be debated.

Nature study in art should not be an imitative reproduction of fortuitous impressions of nature, but rather an analytical, exploratory development and production of the forms and colors needed for true characterization. Such studies do not imitate, but interpret. In order for this interpretation to be pertinent, close observation and clear thinking must precede it. The senses are sharpened, and the artistic intellect is trained in rational analysis of the observed subject matter. The student must take the field against nature, for her powers of presentation are different from and superior to the artist's means of representation. Cézanne worked indefatigably with natural subjects. Van Gogh was destroyed in this struggle, never having compromised his effort to turn his responses to nature into paintings that meaningfully integrated form and color.

Each artist must decide the scope of his nature study, according to his own needs. However, it would be unwise to neglect the external world, from a superabundance of "inner life." We may take warning from the history of India where, out of preoccupation with exalted spiritual fulfillment, mystics forgot that material life, too, demands cultivation and direction. Today, overpopulation and undernourishment are forcing spiritual leaders to concern themselves with the evolution of the family and the economy.

Nature in its rhythm of the seasons, turning now outward, now inward, might well serve as a model for our individual lives. In spring and summer, the forces of earth press outward in growth and maturation; in fall and winter they turn inward and renew themselves.

Let us now consider the problem of colors in nature.

Physically speaking, objects have no color. When white light – by which we mean sunlight – strikes the surface of an object, the latter, according to its molecular constitution, will absorb certain wave lengths, or colors, and reflect others.

In the section on color physics, it was stated that the colors of the spectrum may be divided into two groups in any way, and each group united into one color by means of a converging lens. The resulting two colors are complementary to each other. The rays of light reflected from a surface therefore constitute a color complementary to the color of the absorbed rays. The reflected color appears to us as the intrinsic or local color of the object.

A body that reflects all wave lengths of white light and absorbs none looks white. A body that absorbs all wave lengths of white light and reflects none looks black.

If we illuminate a blue body with orange light, it will look black because orange contains no blue for it to reflect. This demonstrates the primacy of the color of the incident light. Change the color of the lighting, and the local colors of the objects illuminated will change. The more chromatic the lighting, the more the intrinsic colors are modified. The whiter the lighting, the more purely the unabsorbed wave lengths are reflected, and the purer the intrinsic colors appear. Attention to color of illumination is essential in the study of color in nature. We may recall the procedure of the Impressionists who studied the modifications of local colors in continually changing light.

Of course, the intensity of the light is important as well as its color. Light is the cause, not only of the coloration of objects, but also of their plastic corporeality. We shall here distinguish three different intensities, to be called full light, medium light and shadow.

The local color of objects is most effective in medium light, and details of surface texture are most clearly visible. Full light whitens the intrinsic color, while shadow obscures and darkens it.

Colored light reflected from colored objects variously modifies the colors of other objects.

Every colored object reflects its color into the surrounding space. If such an object is red, and if its red light falls upon a nearby white object, the latter will show reddish reflection. If the red rays strike a green object, the latter will show some gray, since green and red extinguish each other. If the red rays strike a black surface, black-brown reflection will appear.

The glossier the surface, the more conspicuous these reflections will be.

The Impressionist painters, in studying the alterations of intrinsic colors by the changing color of sunlight and of reflections, became convinced that local colors are dissolved in a total atmosphere of color.

So we find that we have four main problems to deal with in the study of color impressions – intrinsic color, color of illumination, shadow, and reflection.

An object may be represented in a variety of ways. It may be drawn in top view, front view and side view, to an exact scale of dimensions; this is an analytical form of representation. Then again, an object may be delineated in perspective, or modeled in light and shade.

A red vase and a yellow box may be drawn in perspective and their local colors painted flat (Fig. 136). The shapes and colors may then be modeled with light and shade (Fig. 137). The plastic effect can be flattened again by tying the tonal areas of the objects to the picture plane with tonal areas of like brilliance in the background (Fig. 138).

When each object and each area is assigned its proper local color, a realistic, concrete effect is obtained. The composition of Fig. 139 consists of a multiplicity of elements that only reluctantly unite into a coherent whole. Konrad Witz often made use of this mode.

In Fig. 140, the colors of the objects are introduced into the composition as local colors, each object being set in its own color, red in red, yellow in yellow. The objects are thereby released from their bounded isolation, dissolving into their own atmosphere, which becomes the picture atmosphere.

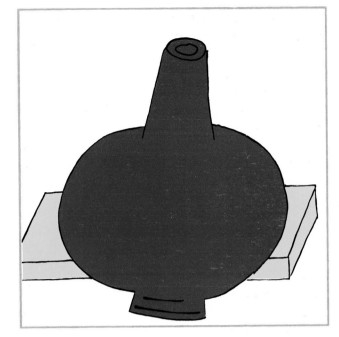

136 · 137 · 138
139 · 140

141

142

Plastic effects may also be obtained by means of cold-warm modulations (Fig. 141). Intrinsic colors begin to be dissolved. Variations of light and shade are replaced by equivalent colder or warmer variations of the local colors. Light-dark contrast is largely eliminated, and an effect of pictorial atmosphere results.

Local colors may be studied as modified by the color of the incident light. In bluish light, a green vase will look blue-green and a yellow dish yellow-green, because the intrinsic colors mix with the hue of the light.

Reflections break up local tones and dissolve the shapes and colors of objects in a polyphony of patches (Fig. 142). A good example of the play of reflections is Renoir's painting "Le Moulin de la Galette," a detail of which was shown in Plate X. Delacroix said that all nature is reflection.

Colored shadows are another topic in the study of color impressions.

When shadows of trees are observed on a summer evening in the orange light of sunset, while the eastern sky is clear, the blue color may be seen very plainly. Colored shadows can be observed still more easily in winter, when snow lies in the streets. Under a dark-blue night sky, in the orange light of street lamps, deep blue, luminous shadows are seen on the snow. Passing along a busy shopping street with many-colored displays after a snow, one may see red, green, blue and yellow shadows on the ground.

In painting, an attack on this problem was made by the Impressionists. Blue shadows of trees in their paintings caused great excitement among visitors at exhibitions. The common opinion had been that shadows should be painted gray-black. But the Impressionists had arrived at the representation of colored shadows by minute observation of nature.

However, the term "impression" as used here is not restricted to the Impressionist school of painting. The Van Eycks, Holbein, Velásquez, Zurbarán, the Le Nain brothers, Chardin and Ingres all painted impressionally in that their works are informed by close observation of nature.

Chinese brush-and-ink painting is also in large part impressional. Characteristic philosophical attitudes involved veneration of nature and natural forces. Not surprisingly, therefore, painters devoted thorough study to the forms of nature. Mountains, water, trees, flowers, became aesthetic symbols. The Chinese painter studies natural forms until he masters them like written characters. To represent these natural forms, he commonly employs but one pigment, black ink, which he modulates in all possible shades. The abstract connotation of black ink intensifies the fundamentally symbolic character of his painting.

In contemporary painting, human faces may show green, blue or violet. People are often at a loss to account for these unnatural colors. There are various reasons that may prompt a painter to use colors in this manner.

Blue and violet in a face may have expressive significance, representing a psychological state. Again, a green or blue face may have symbolic meaning. Such devices are not new. Symbolic complexion is found at an early period in both Indian and Mexican painting. Or, green or blue in a face may represent the shadow effect of a corresponding color of illumination.

The following experiments may help to clarify the problem of colored shadows. In 1944, I had occasion to demonstrate this phenomenon in connection with an exhibition at the Zurich Museum of Arts and Crafts. A white object was illuminated, in daylight, with red light; a green shadow resulted. Green light produced a red shadow, yellow light a violet shadow, and violet light a yellow shadow.

In daylight, each colored light produced a shadow of the complementary color. I asked Hans Finsler, the photographer, to take pictures of this phenomenon. Color photos showed that the colored shadows were really present, and not due simply to simultaneous contrast. All the mixtures of colors in such experiments correspond to additive color syntheses, being mixtures of light rather than of pigments.

In further experiments with colored shadows, the following surprising results were obtained:

1) In red light, in the absence of daylight, a black shadow was produced, as in Fig. 143. Shadows in blue and green illumination were likewise black.

126

2)   The object was illuminated with two colored lights in the absence of daylight. In the case of red and green lights, the red light produced green shadows, and vice versa. The intersection of the two shadows was black, and the mixture of green and red light was yellow. When red-orange and blue-green light was used, the red-orange light produced a blue-green shadow, and vice versa. The intersection of the shadows was black, and the mixture of the two illuminating colors was lavender, as shown in Fig. 144. When the illuminating colors were green and blue, the green light produced a blue shadow, and vice versa. The intersection of the shadows was black, and the mixed light was blue-green.

3)   When three illuminating colors, red-orange, green and blue-green, were used, the result was as shown in Fig. 145. The red-orange light produced a blue-green shadow, the green light produced a lavender shadow, and the blue-green light produced a yellow shadow. The intersection of the three shadows was black. The mixture of the three colored lights produced a white background.

Impressional studies offer the artist many opportunities to interpret the marvels of form and color found in nature.

143

144

145

Plate XXIV
Jean Auguste Dominique Ingres, 1780 - 1867;
Reclining Odalisque.
Paris, the Louvre

Ingres was born in 1780, near the time of the French Revolution, and the naturalism of Jean Jacques Rousseau may have influenced his thinking. His sojourns in Rome and his studies of Greek and Roman masterpieces made him a classicist. The treatment of form and color in the Napoleonic period was one of detached sympathy. David and Ingres represent this period in painting.

An uncommon gift for acute observation and representation established Ingres as the portrait painter of the age. His numerous drawings are especially fine. Ingres explored rhythm and movement in nature with as much care as the Impressionists were to devote to color, half a century later. His development of local colors and shapes is only seemingly photographic; actually, he modified nature to a major degree. Thus the proportions of the figure in our example are modified for the sake of grandiose total effect. The painting of the figure demonstrates the artist's extraordinary visual sensitivity. The effect of his pictures is realistic, not naturalistic. Ingres developed his local and object colors with only seeming fidelity to nature; actually, major departures from nature are undertaken. In the same way, he has greatly modified the odalisque's natural proportions in the direction of a general effect of enlargement. The construction of the picture is considered with great care, and the natural forms are transmuted into pictorial forms. The principal lines of the back and outstretched arm are nearly parallel. The line of the back begins at the uppermost point of the turban and swings in a simple geometric curve through the left foot to the right side of the picture. The curve of the arm continues in a fold of the hanging, up to the top. Both curves are pure abstract line. They are contrasted with strong straight lines and angles.

The color composition is very simple. Blue, orange, brown and yellow are local colors, modulated with black, white and gray. The blue and dark brown of the background and the white of the cloth lend the body the tone of a light mediant. The active forces of the painting are light-dark and saturation contrasts.

The repose of the figure is strongly emphasized by the horizontals, and by the horizontally and vertically penetrating principal color, blue.

Ingres is to be counted, I believe, among the impressional group of painters, since he derived his characteristic qualities from the impressions gained by systematic study from life.

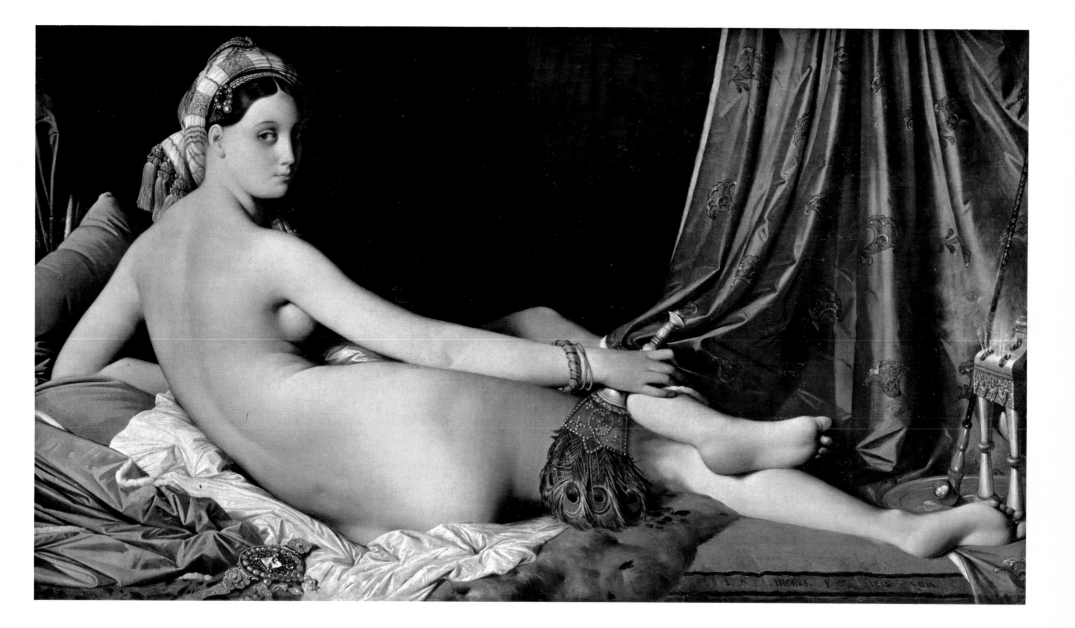

146

147

The optical, electromagnetic and chemical processes initiated in the eye and brain are frequently paralleled by processes in the psychological realm. Such reverberations of the experience of color may be propagated to the inmost centers, thereby affecting principal areas of mental and emotional experience. Goethe spoke of the ethico-aesthetic activity of colors. By careful analysis, I shall try to elucidate this topic, so important to the color artist.

I recall the following anecdote:

A businessman was entertaining a party of ladies and gentlemen at dinner. The arriving guests were greeted by delicious smells issuing from the kitchen, and all were eagerly anticipating the meal. As the happy company assembled about the table, laden with good things, the host flooded the apartment with red light. The meat looked rare and appetizing enough, but the spinach turned black and the potatoes were bright red. Before the guests had recovered from their astonishment, the red light changed to blue, the roast assumed an aspect of putrefaction and the potatoes looked moldy. All the diners lost their appetite at once; but when the yellow light was turned on, transforming the claret into castor oil and the company into living cadavers, some of the more delicate ladies hastily rose and left the room. No one could think of eating, though all present knew it was only a change in the color of the lighting. The host laughingly turned the white lights on again, and soon the good spirits of the gathering were restored. Who can doubt that colors exert profound influences upon us, whether we are aware of them or not?

The deep blue of the sea and distant mountains enchants us; the same blue as an interior seems uncanny, lifeless, and terrifying. Blue reflections on the skin render it pale, as if moribund. In the dark of night, a blue neon light is attractive, like blue on black, and in conjunction with red and yellow lights it lends a cheerful, lively tone. A blue sun-filled sky has an active and enlivening effect, whereas the mood of the blue moonlit sky is passive and evokes subtle nostalgias.

Redness in the face denotes wrath or fever; a blue, green or yellow complexion, sickness, though there is nothing sickly about the pure colors. A red sky threatens bad weather; a blue, green or yellow sky promises fair weather.

On the basis of these experiences of nature, it would seem all but impossible to formulate simple and true propositions about the expressive content of colors.

Yellow shadows, violet light, blue-green fire, red-orange ice, are effects in apparent contradiction with experience, and give an other-worldly expression. Only those deeply responsive can experience the tonal values of single or simultaneous colors without reference to objects. Musical experience is denied to those with no ear for music.

The example of the four seasons, Figs. 146 to 149, shows that color sensation and experience have objective correlatives, even though each individual sees, feels and evaluates color in a very personal way. I have often maintained that the judgment "pleasing-displeasing" can be no valid criterion of true and correct coloration. A serviceable yardstick is obtained only if we base each judgment on the relation and relative position of each color with respect to the adjacent color and the totality of colors. Stated in terms of the four seasons, this means that for each season we are to find those colors, those points on and in the color sphere, that distinctly belong to the expression of that season in their relation to the whole universe of colors.

The youthful, light, radiant generation of nature in Spring is expressed by luminous colors; Fig. 146. Yellow is the color nearest to white light, and yellow-green is its intensification. Light pink and light blue tones amplify and enrich the chord. Yellow, pink and lilac are often seen in the buds of plants.

The colors for Autumn contrast most sharply with those of Spring. In Autumn, the green of vegetation dies out, to be broken down and decomposed into dull brown and violet; Fig. 148.

The promise of Spring is fulfilled in the maturity of Summer.

Nature in Summer, thrust materially outward into a maximum luxuriance of form and color, attains extreme density and a vividly plastic fullness of powers. Warm, saturated, active colors, to be found at their peak in only one particular region of the color sphere, offer themselves for the expression of Summer; Fig. 147. For contrast with and amplification of these principal colors, their complements will of course also be required.

To represent Winter, typifying passivity in nature by a contracting, inward movement of the forces of earth, we require colors connoting withdrawal, cold and centripetal radiance, transparency, rarefaction; Fig. 149.

148

149

The majestic cycle of respiration performed by nature in these four phases can hence be clearly and objectively represented in color; but unless we apply reason to the choice of color combinations, keeping the total universe of color before us, we shall find none but private solutions, and miss those of general truth and validity.

In order to gain an understanding of each hue in its unique psychological, expressive value, let us relate it to the other hues. To avoid error insofar as possible, we must know, when mentioning any color, precisely what chroma and what tone are meant, and with what color it is to be related. When I say "red," I must specify which red, as well as the color to be related to it. A yellowish red, such as red-orange, is different in species from a bluish red, and red-orange on lemon-yellow is again a very different matter from red-orange on black, or on its equal in brilliance, lilac.

I shall now try to relate the hues yellow, red, blue, orange, violet and green as represented and defined in the 12-hue color circle of Fig. 37, and to describe their mental and emotional expressive values.

Yellow

Yellow is the most light-giving of all hues. It loses this trait the moment we shade it with gray, black or violet. Yellow is, as it were, a denser, material white. The further this yellowed light is drawn into the denseness of matter, of opacity, the more it is assimilated to yellow-orange, orange and red-orange. Our red is the stopping point of yellow, with which it is not visibly tinged. In the center of the yellow-to-red band, we have orange, as the strongest and most concentrated interpenetration of light and matter. Golden yellow suggests the highest sublimation of matter by the power of light, impalpably radiant, lacking transparency, but weightless as a pure vibration. Gold was formerly much used in painting. It signifies luminous, light-emitting matter. The golden domes of Byzantine mosaics and the backgrounds in the paintings of early masters were symbols of the beyond, the marvelous, the kingdom of sun and light. The golden aura of saints is the token of their transfiguration. The attainment of this state was conceived as an envelopment by light. This heavenly light could not be symbolized except by gold.

In common speech, to "see the light" means to be brought to a realization of previously hidden truth. To say that someone is "bright" is to credit him with intelligence. So yellow, the brightest and lightest color, pertains symbolically to understanding, knowledge. In Grünewald's conception, the risen Christ ascends in a glory of yellow. Yellow is used in the sense of celestial light in Altdorfer's "Madonna and Child with Angels."

Just as there is but one truth, so there is only one yellow. Adulterated truth is vitiated truth, untruth. So the expressions of diluted yellow are envy, betrayal, falseness, doubt, distrust and unreason. In Giotto's "Taking of Christ" and in Holbein's "Last Supper," Judas is shown in dim yellow. The gray-yellow cloak of a female figure in the "Stripping of Christ" by El Greco has a peculiarly mistrustful effect.

On the other hand, yellow is radiantly cheerful when contrasted with dark tones.

Figs. 150 - 153 show how the same yellow may be altered in expression by different juxtaposed colors. Fig. 150 shows yellow on white. The yellow looks dark and rayless. The white thrusts it into a subordinate position. If the yellow and white are interchanged, both assume a different expression.

Fig. 151 shows yellow on light pink. Simultaneous effect shifts it towards greenish yellow, and its radiant power is subdued. Where pure love (pink) chiefly reigns, reason and knowledge (yellow) seem to languish.

Yellow on orange itself acts as a purer, lighter orange. The two colors together are like strong morning sun on ripening wheatfields.

Fig. 152 shows yellow on green. The yellow radiates outward, outshining the green. Since green is a mixture of yellow and blue, the yellow is among friends.

Yellow on red-violet has an extreme and characteristic power, hard and inexorable. But when yellow is mixed with red-violet, it loses its character immediately, becoming sickly, brownish and indifferent.

Yellow on medium blue is radiant but alien and repellent in effect. Sentimental blue will not readily tolerate the bright wit of yellow.

Yellow on red is a loud joyful noise, like trumpets on Easter Morn. Its splendor sends forth a mighty knowledge and affirmation.

Fig. 153 shows yellow on black, in its brightest and most aggressive luminosity. It is vigorous and sharp, uncompromising and abstract.

Figs. 150 - 153 clearly illustrate the various effects of yellow and the difficulty of defining the expressive properties of a color in general terms without relating it to other colors.

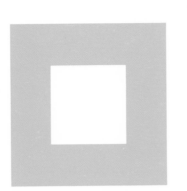

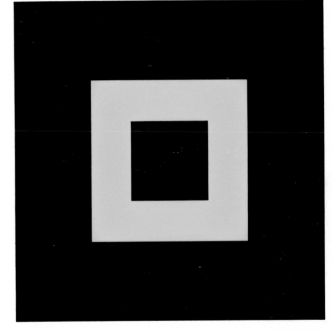

150 · 151
152 · 153

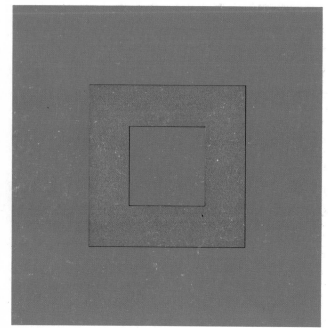

154 · 155
156 · 157

Red

The red of the 12-hue color circle is neither yellowish nor bluish. Its irresistible radiancy is not easily eclipsed, and yet is extraordinarily flexible, bordering on diverse characters. It is very sensitive where it shifts into yellowish or into bluish. Both yellowish red and bluish red unfold great capacity for modulation.

Red-orange is dense and opaque, glowing as if filled with inner warmth. The warmness of red is intensified to fiery strength in red-orange. It is symbolically comparable to vitalized earth. Red-orange light promotes vegetable growth and organic function.

Proper contrasting turns red-orange into an expression of feverish, belligerent passion. Associated with the planet Mars, red is bound to the burning worlds of war and demons. It was worn as a sign of martial occupation by warriors in combat. It has been the badge of revolutions.

Passionate physical love glows forth in red-orange; blue-red purple connotes spiritual love. Thus Charonton portrayed the Father and the Son in crimson robes (Plate II). The Madonna of the Isenheim altarpiece and the Madonna of Stuppach, by Grünewald, are both clad in red.

In purple, the color of the cardinals, temporal and spiritual power are united.

By varying color contrasts with red-orange, I try to show in Figs. 154 - 157 how a red may be expressively modified.

Fig. 154: On lemon yellow, the red shows a dark, subdued force. It is dominated by the force of yellow, of knowledge.

In Fig. 155, red on dark pink acts with quiet, extinguishing heat.

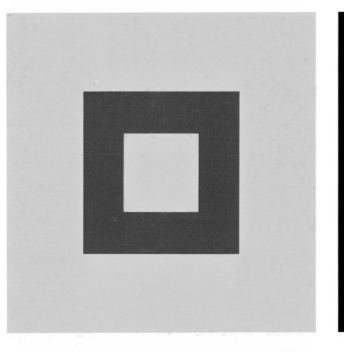
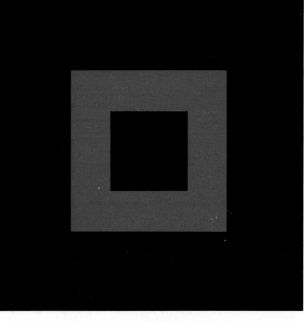

On green-blue, the red is like a blazing fire (Fig. 156).

On lilac, it drops back to a subdued glow, and drives the lilac to active resistance (Fig. 157).

On yellow-green, the red is an impudent, rash intruder, loud and common.

On orange, red seems smoldering, dark and lifeless, as if parched. If the orange is deepened to dark brown, the red fire flares with a dry heat.

It is only in contrast with black that red-orange develops its utmost unconquerable, demonic passion.

The different effects of red-orange in our examples are only a suggestion of its expressive potentialities. Unlike yellow, red has a great wealth of modulations because it can be widely varied between cold and warm, dull and clear, light and dark, without destroying its character of redness. From demonic, sinister red-orange on black, to sweet angelic pink, red can express all intermediate degrees between the infernal and the sublime. Only the ethereal, transparent, aerial is barred to it, for there blue reigns supreme.

Blue

Pure blue is a color containing no trace of yellow or red.

As red is always active, so blue is always passive, from the point of view of material space. From the point of view of spiritual immateriality, blue seems active and red passive. Blue is always cold, and red is always warm. Blue is contracted, introverted. As red is associated with blood, so is blue with the nervous system.

Blue is a power like that of nature in winter, when all germination and growth is hidden in

158 · 159
160 · 161

darkness and silence. Blue is always shadowy, and tends in its greatest glory to darkness. It is an intangible nothing, and yet present as the transparent atmosphere. In the atmosphere of the earth, blue appears from lightest azure to the deepest blue-black of the night sky. Blue beckons our spirit with the vibrations of faith into the infinite distances of spirit. Signifying faith to us, for the Chinese it symbolized immortality.

When blue is dimmed, it falls into superstition, fear, grief and perdition, but always it points to the realm of the transcendental.

Figs. 158 - 161 show changes in the effect of blue with changing color contrast.

Fig. 158 shows blue as a dark color on yellow. Its effect is very dark indeed, and devoid of radiance. Where bright intellect rules, faith appears dull and obscure. When the blue is lightened to the same brilliance as the yellow, it casts a cold light. Its transparency demotes yellow to a dense, material hue.

Fig. 159 shows blue on black. Here it gleams in bright, pure strength. Where black ignorance holds sway, the blue of pure faith shines like a distant light.

If we set blue on lilac, as in Fig. 160, it appears withdrawn, inane and impotent. The lilac takes from it all significance by right of the greater material strength of "practical faith." When the lilac is darkened, the blue takes back its luster.

On dark brown (dark, dull orange), blue is excited into a strong vibrant tremor, and the brown simultaneously awakens into live color. The brown that was dead is resurrected by the power of blue.

Blue on red-orange retains its dark figure, yet becomes luminous, asserting and maintaining its strange unreality.

Fig. 161 shows that on quiet green, our blue is markedly displaced towards red. Only by this "evasion" can it escape from the paralyzing saturation of the green and return to active life.

The retiring nature of blue, its meekness and profound faith, are frequently encountered in paintings of the Annunciation. The Virgin, hearkening inward, wears blue. A fine example is in Roger van der Weyden's Altar of the Epiphany.

The garment of Christ in Grünewald's "Derision of Jesus" is an arresting light blue. In the sureness of bright faith, He endures the insults of the unknowing in utter passivity. Nearly the same color of blue is worn by St. Anthony in the "Temptation" of the Isenheim altarpiece.

Green

Green is the intermediate between yellow and blue. According as green contains more yellow or more blue, the character of its expression changes. Green is one of the secondary colors, produced by mixing two primaries — an operation difficult to perform in such a way that neither component predominates.

Green is the color of the vegetable kingdom, the mysterious chlorophyll involved in photosynthesis. When light comes to the earth, and water and air release their elements, then incarnate sentience puts forth green. Fruitfulness and contentment, tranquility and hope are expressive values of green, the fusion and interpenetration of knowledge and faith. When luminous green is dulled by gray, a sense of sad decay easily results. If the green inclines towards yellow, coming within the range of yellow-green, we feel the young, vernal force of nature. A spring or early summer morning without yellow-green, without hope and joy for the fruits of summer, is unthinkable.

Yellow-green may be activated to the utmost by orange, though it then readily assumes a coarse, vulgar cast.

If the green inclines towards blue, its spiritual components are augmented. Manganese blue represents the richest hue of blue-green. This ice blue is the cold pole, as red-orange is the warm pole, of our color world. In antithesis to green and blue, it has a cold, vigorous aggressiveness.

The range of modulation of green is very broad, and many different expressive values can be obtained by variations in contrast.

Orange

Orange, the mixture of yellow and red, is at the focus of maximum radiant activity. It has solar luminosity in the material sphere, attaining the maximum of warm, active energy in reddish orange. Festive orange readily becomes proud external ostentation. Whitened, it quickly loses character; diluted with black, it declines into dull, taciturn and withered brown. By lightening brown, we obtain beige tones, engendering a warm, beneficent atmosphere in quiet, intimate interiors.

Violet

The difficulty of fixing a precise violet, neither reddish nor bluish, is extreme. Many individuals have no discrimination for shades of violet. As the antipode of yellow, or consciousness, violet is the color of the unconscious – mysterious, impressive and sometimes oppressive, now menacing, now encouraging, according to contrast. When violet is present in large areas it can be distinctly terrifying, particularly towards the purple. "A light of this kind, cast upon a landscape," says Goethe, "suggests the terrors of the end of the world."

Violet is the hue of piety, and, when darkened and dulled, of dark superstition. Lurking catastrophe bursts forth from dark violet. Once it is lightened, when light and understanding illuminate dark piety, delicate and lovely tints enchant us.

Chaos, death and exaltation in violet, solitude and dedication in blue-violet, divine love and spiritual dominion in red-violet – these, in few words, are some of the expressive values of the violet band. Many plants have light violet shoots with yellow centers.

Generally speaking, all tints represent the brighter aspects of life, whereas shades symbolize the dark and negative forces.

We can use two tests to check the accuracy of these remarks on the expressive values of colors. If two colors are complementary, their interpretations should be complementary; and when a color is mixed, its interpretation should correspond to the mixture of the interpretations of the original colors.

1. Complementary Pairs
   yellow : violet = bright knowledge : dark, emotional piety
   blue : orange = submissive faith : proud self-respect
   red : green = material force : sympathy

2. Mixed Colors
   red + yellow = orange
   power + knowledge = proud self-respect
   red + blue = violet
   love + faith = piety
   yellow + blue = green
   knowledge + faith = compassion

The more I consider the mentally and emotionally expressive values of colors, the more I realize that the effects of colors and our subjective individuality in receptiveness to color experience are both extremely variable.

Any color may be varied in five modes:

1) In hue; that is, green may become more yellowish or more bluish, orange more yellowish or reddish, etc.

2) In brilliance; that is, red may appear as pink, red, dark red, and blue as light blue, blue, dark blue, etc.

3) In saturation; that is, blue may be more or less diluted with white, black, gray or its complementary (orange).

4) In extension; a large area of green may lie beside a small area of yellow, or vice versa, or the quantities of yellow and green may be equal.

5) In effects due to simultaneous contrast.

The contents of this section have brought us to a critical point in the process of artistic creation. Perception and experience may be keen, but unless the proper basic group is selected from the totality of colors at the outset, the final effect of the work is jeopardized. Therefore, subconscious perception, intuitive thought and positive knowledge should always function together, enabling us to choose appropriately from the multiplicity of means available.

Matisse's sketch, Fig. 36, illustrates his practice of organizing his colors in advance. He himself wrote, "Given a correct fundamental attitude, it would turn out that the procedure of making a picture is no less logical than that of building a house. The human aspect need not be considered. One has it or not; if one has it, it will show up in the work anyway."

The following are some examples which show how expressive values of colors have been utilized by painters.

In the Basle Art Museum there are some paintings by Konrad Witz. They differ sharply in coloration, and bring out the expressions we have ascribed to the various hues. Witz is one of those painters who are objectively precise in their use of color, rather than subjectively biased.

One of these paintings is "Caesar and Antipater." Caesar has summoned his accused general to give an account of himself. Antipater is excitedly protesting his innocence. His gaping cloak is glowing hot red-orange, like fever, while Caesar, in the consciousness of his authority, wears a cold, dark blue-green. This icy color is highly effective because the throne on which Caesar is sitting encloses the chill of his reserve in complementary red-orange. The gold border of the blue-green mantle is painted in yellow and black, the yellow striking sharp and hard, like the words of Caesar.

Another subject, "David and Abishai," shows David standing in royal purple against a complementary green, receiving a gift from the respectfully kneeling Abishai. The effect of the picture is extremely calm, David's vertical figure being in equilibrium with the horizontal green.

Plate XXV
Konrad Witz, 1410 - 1445;
The Synagogue.
Basle, Kunstmuseum

Konrad Witz elaborated two distinct components of pictorial design in his paintings.

In the first place, he chose to give each subject an appropriate and unmistakable expression by means of coloration. He used color as the vehicle for ideational content. Each of his pictures is therefore constructed on a particular chord proper to it alone.

In the second place, Witz's later paintings place the expressively colored figures in perspective space. This space presents many antitheses of direction. The architecture is rendered in perspective down to minute details, and modeled in dull, neutral tints and shades. The luminous colors of the people in these scenes are what lends his work its characteristic features. The representation of people also exhibits plastic elements. Folds of garments are often fashioned to give an effect of abstract texture.

In this painting, Witz ascribes a yellow dress to the Synagogue personified as a woman. The folds parallel the architecture. The lady is standing in a space of dark gray, the open door of which discloses a blue-green depth. In her right arm she bears two Tables of the Law, and her left hand holds a broken staff. The yellow of her dress symbolizes the rational, logical thought and philosophical learning of the Jews. Contrast of the light yellow with the dark gray background imparts a special expression to the yellow. In the illuminated part of the dress, the yellow is modulated with gray-violet tones of a similar brilliance. These modulations transform the yellow into a living, vibrant chord of simultaneous resonance. Witz develops the shadow tones in the warm red-orange of the sleeves. This red-orange is complementary to the blue-green through the door. The staff is broken back at the point where it reaches the doorway. The Synagogue appears to intend to pass the threshold, but her staff is broken; she cannot advance the banner and lead the people into the Land of Promise, symbolized as a distant aspiration by the blue-green color. The scarcely visible veil before her eyes and the tablets held in her arm symbolize blind veneration of law.

The gray-brown background colors, the yellow, red-orange and blue-green mixtures, intensify the tragic, melancholy expression of the work.

Plate XXVI
Pieter Bruegel the Elder, 1525-1569;
Parable of the Blind Men.
Naples, Museo Nazionale

From the upper left of the picture, a procession of six blind men declines diagonally to the lower right. They stagger along in three groups of two. The foremost man, already fallen, matches the colors of water and soil. Only his white-stockinged shins thrust forth, forming a triplet with the white leg of the second in line, and related to his white cap and the clear view through the tree immediately above. The falling second man's red-violet sleeve is attracted to the purple of the fallen man's vest, and the association is pulling him down. The light blue-violet of his tabard together with the white of cap and legs supports a chill, deathly expression. Piety (violet) proved useless to the blind fool with the cap; he fell into the ditch with the leader.

The next group, the third and the fourth blind man, is highly agitated, with rhythms of flapping fabrics and excited gestures. The third man, in dim blue-gray under a light gray cape, matching the shades of the church in the background, is extending his left arm forward, and the hand, holding the staff, is perpendicularly beneath the steeple, as if balancing it. His lost eyes are raised at the church; to no avail. He sees nothing, but holds on by the stick of Number Two, tumbling before him. He is a devout egotist, well provided with all things needful.

The fourth is losing hold of his falling staff and hopefully (green jacket) grasping the shoulder of the third. His jacket and purple stockings connect him to the colors of the first man, and his gray-violet cloak to the second. He courts the same disaster as the leaders.

The dark blue-gray cloak of Number Five divides the middle pair from the last. He is hesitant, dependent and superstitious (blue-gray); he has a rosary with crucifix about the neck. His purple jerkin, again, connects him with the first and fourth. The sixth and last is merely stout, dull and simple. The color of his outer garment blends wholly with the sheen of the ditch water at the lower left. He may fall anywhere.

This sorry train, in its shadowless incorporeality, has a ghostly, unreal effect. The light violet/gray/blue-gray/white coloration with the complementary ocher of the earth, the purple with the green, is quite unusual with Bruegel, whose other paintings never use tragic light violet and blue-gray so prominently. To us this means that Bruegel chose the colors for the sake of their expressive values.

Folling

Grünewald painted each subject with ruthless candor and unprecedented force and clarity. He exploded all conventional precepts of coloration, and strove for a universal symbolism. Each scene was most sharply individualized in both form and color. When these scenes were accessible to view in the coordinated groups of the altar as a whole, a spiritual cohesion and a certain unity were present. As exhibited today, the panels are viewed individually in succession, and no strong interdependence or unity is apparent. Each beholder must reconstruct the total effect for himself. Evidently, Grünewald abstained from any outward, deliberate, decorative unity in favor of a true representation and characterization of particular themes.

Our example shows the "Resurrection and Transfiguration." This composition begins at the lower left with the hand and sword of a watchman, transverse to his person, which is rhythmically turned in high contrast. This figure appears parallel to the picture plane. The second watchman is recumbent, transverse to the first, extending into the foreground. Behind this group is a horizontal sarcophagus. The first watchman's right foot, or rather the bright area beside it, points back to the third, kneeling watchman, bowing himself forward. Behind him kneels a fourth, in countermovement with the third. The entire lower portion of the picture is filled with sharply contrasting movements.

As to color, we see an isolated strong yellow in the clothes of the first watchman, the second shows dark red, the sarcophagus red-orange, and the third watchman flaming patches of red. The gleam of the sword hilt in the left corner finds counter-accents in the helmet of the first watchman and the head of the third watchman. These three points make a supine acute triangle filled with tension in the direction of depth. The hand on the sword hilt is the apex of an angle formed by the blade and a vertical line crossing the breast to the left elbow. This angle opens like a chalice, whence the movement of the pall pours upward. Shining uneasily undulating, the shroud runs diagonally up the picture, and from this there is detached, in slightly leftward motion, the figure of the Arisen, suspended in an aura of triumphal size.

The diagonal movement of the cloth is kept in the picture plane by the mighty, cross-laid, red-brown rock. Grünewald unfolds the whole metaphysical power of the color universe in the pall and aura. From the dull, earthy dark-red of the watchman, he picks out the complementary light-green in the flickering shroud, and thence passes through dark-green, blue-green, blue, blue-violet, violet, red-violet, red, red-orange, and orange, to yellow and white in the body of Christ, traversing the whole spectral cycle at its most luminous. The light red-orange and pink of the aura contrast with a complementary ice-blue circlet. It is all one mighty and inclusive chord, beginning almost colorlessly, then swelling and soaring heavenward.

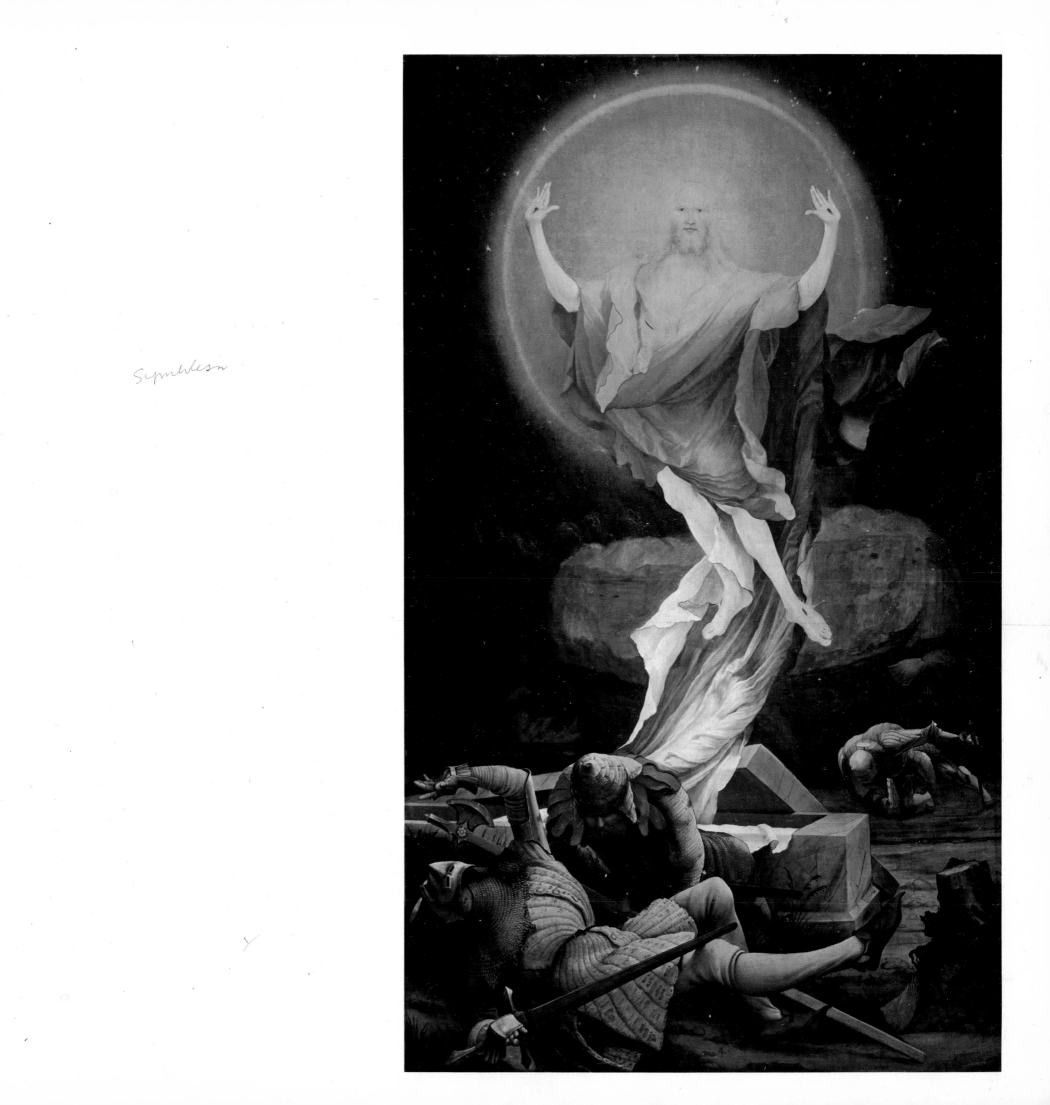

COMPOSITION

To compose in color means to juxtapose two or more colors in such a way that they jointly produce a distinct and distinctive expression. The selection of hues, their relative situation, their locations and orientations within the composition, their configurations or simultaneous patterns, their extensions and their contrast relationships, are decisive factors of expression.

The subject of color composition is so many-faceted that we shall only be able to suggest some of the basic ideas.

Some of the resources for harmonious composition were discussed in the section on harmony. In interpreting the expressive properties of colors (section on color expression), we have tried to state concrete conditions and requirements for the genesis of one characteristic expression or another. The purpose to be served by means of colors must govern their selection.

It is an essential point that the effect of a color is determined by its situation relative to accompanying colors. A color is always to be seen in relation to its surroundings.

In Figs. 162 and 163, yellow and green are each associated with four colors of the same brilliance; light-dark contrast has been eliminated.

In Fig. 162, blue-violet and red-violet, nearly complementary to yellow, are the most intense, while green and light orange, neighbors to yellow in the spectrum, are comparatively inactive.

In Fig. 163, the most intense is red, the complementary of green, while blue-green and yellow-green, the tertiary derivatives of green, are feeble.

The farther a hue is removed from a given hue in the color circle, the greater its power of contrast.

However, the value and importance of a color in the picture are not determined by the accompanying colors alone. Quality and quantity of extension are contributing factors.

Thus the placement and direction of colors is important in pictorial composition. Blue behaves differently at the top, bottom, left or right of the field. Low blue is heavy, high blue is light. Dark red at the top acts as a heavy, impending weight; at the bottom, as a stable matter of fact. Yellow gives an effect of weightlessness at the top, and of captive buoyancy at the bottom.

To bring about a balance of color distribution is one of the most important aims of composition. As the fulcrum is necessary to the beam of a pair of scales in order to sustain equilibrium, so the vertical axis of equilibrium is essential in a painting. The weights of color areas act on either side of that axis.

In seeking to decide the values of "left" and "right" in a picture, we think first of the human body. The left side is ordinarily, the more passive, the right connoting activity. Right tends onward and upward, while left draws backward and downward. Many paintings begin with accents at the lower left, the movement running towards the upper right. The movement from upper left to lower right in Brueghel's "Parable of the Blind Men," Plate XXVI, is provocative because it runs counter to our habit of looking at a picture. If the blind men were passing from upper right to lower left, we should be tempted to see them in an ascending sequence, and the expression of falling would be lost. This can easily be verified by projecting a laterally inverted image of the picture.

162

163

It may be that my notion of right and left is not valid for left-handed observers. It would also be of value to inquire whether peoples who write and read from right to left or from the top down experience these values correspondingly.

Each of the several possible directions in the field of a painting – horizontal, vertical, diagonal, circular, or combinations of these – has its peculiar expression. "Horizontal" denotes weight, distance, breadth. "Vertical," the strongest antithesis to horizontal, denotes lightness, height and depth. The two directions together give an effect of area, a feeling of equilibrium, solidity and material hardness. A strong accent occurs where horizontal and vertical intersect.

"Diagonal" directions generate movement and lead into the depth of the picture. In Grünewald's "Resurrection," the diagonal motion of the shroud throws the gaze from the horizontal foreground up to the perfection of the aura.

Painters of the Baroque period used diagonals in their murals to produce perspective illusions. El Greco, Liss and Maulpertsch, who developed the expressive moment of their paintings out of directional contrasts of forms and colors, preferred diagonal orientation.

Chinese painters have made conscious use of diagonal movement along with vertical axes to lead the eye into the depths of a landscape, the diagonals often vanishing in misty distance.

The Cubists used diagonal orientation and triangular forms quite differently, to intensify an effect of plastic relief.

"Circular" forms have a concentrating effect, while at the same time producing a feeling of movement. We recall Charonton's "Coronation of

the Virgin," Plate II. The composition of the central structure is circular. Mary's head is the center of the large circle, concentrating the action upon the coronation.

Another excellent example of circular movement is the treatment of the cloud formations in Alt-dorfer's "Victory of Alexander." They repeat and intensify the excitement of the battle scene.

Two or more colors can move in either like or contrary direction. The color diagrams referred to below only represent the principal color orientations. They are not intended as analyses of the paintings.

Fig. 164 shows three colorsplaced side-by-side horizontally. An example of such a composition is Cézanne's landscape in Plate XV. The brown-violet, the green and blue planes, are horizontal. The various orange patches in the green plane are likewise horizontally oriented. This directionality gives the landscape its expression of great expanse.

Fig. 164 viewed sidewise shows three colors in vertical arrangement. Thus in the Picasso still life, Plate VII, the principal blue form and the black and white surfaces are vertically parallel. The principal figures in El Greco's "Stripping of Christ," Plate XVII, define the vertical in purple, yellow and blue-gray.

The exercise of Fig. 165 shows red, blue and yellow horizontally, and green vertically. This set of contrasts produces intersections which become points of rest.

Plate I, from the "Apocalypse de Saint Sever," shows background horizontals of red, blue and yellow, intersected by the erect figures in red, blue and green.

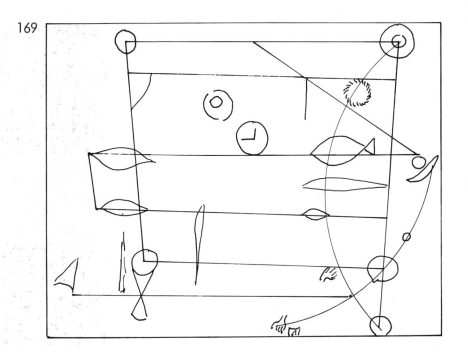

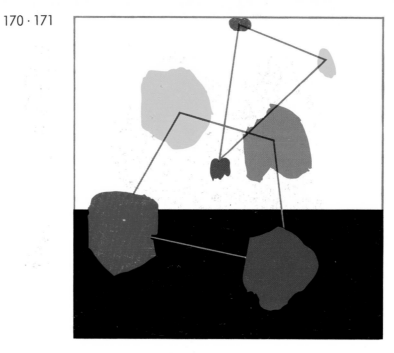

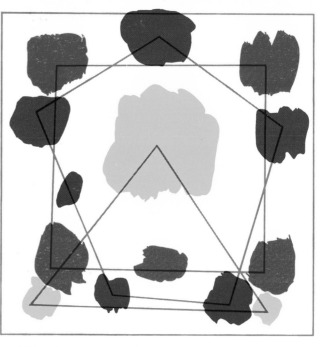

"The Synagogue" by Konrad Witz, Plate XXV, is another example of clearly contrasting horizontals and verticals. The red sleeves and banner are horizontal, while the blue-green opening of the door and the yellow garment are vertical.

Many of Titian's paintings modulate the brilliance of colors in horizontal and vertical directions. This distribution of light and dark has therefore been referred to as "Titian's formula." Figures are introduced in diagonal or circular movement, Fig. 167.

In Seurat's "La Grande Jatte," Plate XXIII, the dark shadow below is diagonal, whereas the dark of the foliage emphasizes the horizontal. The vertical figures are in contrast with these orientations; Fig. 166.

In Van Gogh's "Café at Evening," Plate XVIII, yellow and orange are set off from blue and black horizontally, vertically and diagonally; Fig. 168.

Human vision is such that we tend to join like to like, and see them jointly. The likeness may be of colors, areas, shades, textures or accents. During observation, a visual "configuration" is formed. I call this configuration a simultaneous pattern when it results from the presented relations of likeness, without being itself materially present.

Fig. 170 shows two simultaneous patterns, generated with two sizes of areas and different colors.

Fig. 171 illustrates how the eye tends to see like colors together, and how several simultaneous patterns may coexist when the colors are many. The

172

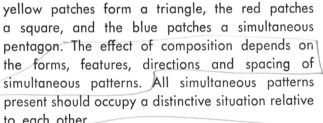

yellow patches form a triangle, the red patches a square, and the blue patches a simultaneous pentagon. The effect of composition depends on the forms, features, directions and spacing of simultaneous patterns. All simultaneous patterns present should occupy a distinctive situation relative to each other.

The fact that likenesses generate simultaneous patterns is a principle of order and articulation. Just as human society is articulated into relationships of blood, opinion or status, so relationships are the source of order and clear intelligibility in a picture. A model composition in this sense is Cézanne's "Apples and Oranges," Plate XII.

In Paul Klee's "Magic Fish," Plate XXI, we find two striking configurations. The large, nearly square configuration lends the picture a static purchase; its right and left sides serve as axes about which the several forms are grouped. The narrow rectangular configuration in the centerline of the picture brackets the group of fish. Without these organizing configurations, the composition would be a chaos of forms; Fig. 169.

Another way to achieve order in a picture is to organize light and dark or cold and warm color groups into well-defined areas and masses. Clear and distinct arrangement and distribution of the principal contrasts is essential to good composition.

A most important element of order is codirectionality or parallelism. This can be used to interconnect complexes of very different kinds.

When colors are used as masses or areas, they can be intensified by the device known as "displacement." In Fig. 172, red and green are presented in two masses. The red is shifted towards green, and the green towards red. Care must be taken that displacements do not disintegrate unified masses or areas and destroy the basic conception. An impressive example of displacement is Cézanne's "La Montagne Ste.-Victoire," Plate XV.

An important consideration is whether a color form shall be statically fixed in effect, or dynamic, free-floating. In Fig. 173, the blue form is free-floating and detached. In Fig. 174, the same form is fixed to the edge of the picture at the left and right. It might instead have been fixed to the top and bottom, or to the top only. This sort of attachment has been called "permeation" by a form or color. In murals, this permeation is very useful for stabilizing the composition. It is especially apparent as a principle of composition in Giotto's frescoes. Much the same stabilization can be achieved by emphasizing a vertical or horizontal within the interior of an unattached form. The vertical or horizontal connects with the boundaries of the picture by parallelism, giving a feeling of static solidity. Pictures constructed in this way seem like self-contained universes. But when such isolation from the surroundings is not wanted, and the painting is to be connected to the world outside and to the infinity of forms and colors, then the boundary must not be accentuated, and the composition should be in a high degree non-directional and frameless. A good example is Monet's "Houses of Parliament in Fog," Plate XI. Some Tachiste paintings also exemplify the principle.

Many different resources of color composition have been suggested. In the execution of a pictorial idea, however, the flow of intuition should not be dammed up by rigid prescription.

This Sienese color composition is most instructive as an example of the significance of directional antitheses in composition, which it conspicuously illustrates. Red permeates horizontally; it is the field in which blue and white are interspersed. Diagonal blue and green lead to the violet center. Violet is the composite of red and blue. The gold-brown clad saint stands before this violet background. Red, blue and violet proclaim that he is preaching of sacred and profane love. Violet and blue lend an atmosphere of simple faith, and white, the color of purity, is stressed. Despite the loving, gentle discourse, the heads of some youths and maidens, and no doubt their hearts too, are turned towards each other, and seem more occupied by temporal affections. The red of their dress is brightened here and there to earthy red-orange.

The worthies on the dais are singly emphasized and identified as personages in compact color shapes, whereas the kneeling men and women are represented en masse. No isolated individuals stand out; the multitude is resolved into insubstantial color patches or patterns. Even the self-conscious, supercilious young bystander at the right is distinguished only by his light brocade robe.

The few distinct hues in the picture carry great power of expression. Natural forms are transmuted into quasi-abstract pictorial forms. The manner in which the color shapes systematically "dematerialize" the shapes of objects testifies to great contrapuntal skill and wise command of plastic resources.

POSTSCRIPT

In this book I have tried to build a serviceable conveyance in which the color artist may travel a longish distance upon his way. Yet this will be no easy pilgrimage. The route is fixed by the inexorable laws of color.

These laws shine forth in the rainbow, and are discernible in the artificially constructed color sphere, extending and enlarging the pure hues and their mixtures into the polar regions of black and white.

Black, with its profound obscurity, is necessary in order to set the beams of colored light in a dimension suitable to them. The bright radiance of white is necessary, lending the colors its material strength.

Between black and white, there throbs the universe of chromatic phenomena. So long as colors are bound to the world of objects, we can perceive them and recognize their relationships; their inner essence remains concealed from our understanding, and must be grasped intuitively. Hence rules and formulae can be no more than signposts on the way to color fulfillment in art.

In his Trattato della Pittura, which sets up a formidable array of rules for painters, Leonardo remarks, "Didst thou attempt to create by rule, thou shouldst accomplish nought, but devise only confusion." Thus he relieved his readers once more of the encumbrance of knowledge, and encouraged them to follow their intuition.

It is not the means of expression and representation that count in art, but the individual in his identity and humanity. First comes the cultivation and creation of the individual; then the individual can create.

The serious study of colors is an excellent means to the cultivation of human beings, for it leads to a perception of inner necessities. To grasp these is to experience the eternal law of all natural generation; to recognize necessity is to surrender self-will and serve the Creator – to become Man.

In this book, I have discussed a number of masterpieces of painting and tried to discover their hidden meanings. I chose old masters chiefly, because many readers may be familiar with the originals. But the color principles they illustrate are timeless, and as valid today as they ever were.

Whoever sees only the subjective and the symbolic content in the paintings of Francesca, Rembrandt, Brueghel, Cézanne, and other masters old and new, to him the gates are closed upon their artistic power and beauty. The end and aim of all artistic endeavor is liberation of the spiritual essence of form and color and its release from imprisonment in the world of objects. It is from this aspiration that non-objective art has arisen. The world we live in today is unlike that known to man in 1560, or 1860. Our world is fashioned by contrivance. We build machines whose meaning lies in their function. Machines are not symbols of ideas, but embodiments of purposeful thought.

Even pictures, today, are not symbolic. They have their raison d'être in themselves, in their forms and colors. The painter uses areas and colors for his own projection; the necessary life force flows from himself. He fashions his experience under the guidance of intuition, or inspiration.

However painting may evolve, color will remain its prime material.

152

ACKNOWLEDGMENT

To the new 1973 edition

When the plans for this book were at the stage of discussion between Mr. Peter Maier and myself, he already fully appreciated the technical difficulties involved in so ambitious an undertaking. As a result of his courageous decision, the publishers have worked indefatigably to make my experience of color available to a larger audience beyond the classroom. I am grateful to the publishing house of Otto Maier for their faith in my project and for their splendid cooperation. Members of the staff were consistently helpful in dealing skillfully with the many problems that arose.

The Graphische Anstalt E. Wartelsteiner, of Munich, has devoted the most painstaking attention to color fidelity in the reproduction of the illustrations.*)

Mrs. Lucia Moholy has been of valuable aid to me in the editing of the manuscript.

This book could never have been completed without the unfailing assistance and encouragement of my wife.

Zurich, February 18, 1961.

Johannes Itten.

When preparing the first edition of "The Art of Color" in 1960, author and publisher faced the difficult problem of finding the best way of reproducing the color. This could only be achieved by producing the various color illustrations and tables in different printing processes done by several printers - partly with special colors - and tipping them in the book.

In 1970, when the students' edition was planned, this complicated method of production could not be retained. Thanks to advanced technology, the printing quality of the students' edition was in many ways an improvement over the large edition. Thus, a standard was set for a new large edition. For the present new printing, the entire production was adapted for offset.

The reproduction of all the illustrations was done by Seiler & Jehle, Augsburg, without whose valuable collaboration the book could not have appeared in its present form. We gratefully acknowledge here this accomplishment, as well as the excellent printing by J. Fink, Stuttgart-Kemnat.

All together, care was taken to leave the work untouched. Contents and sequence of pages have been retained, some of the illustrations enlarged and improved according to existing copies. The aim of the new edition is to make Johannes Itten's color theory available again, improved and strictly adhering to his principles of presentation.

Zurich, April 1973

Anneliese Itten

*) The reproductions for the new 1973 edition were made by Seiler & Jehle, Augsburg.

SOURCES OF PAINTINGS, PHOTOGRAPHS AND REPRODUCTIONS

Plate I (Page 39)
From manuscript "Apocalypse de Saint Sever"
Service Photographique,
Bibliothèque Nationale, Paris

Plate II (Page 41)
Enguerrand Charonton: "Coronation of the Virgin"
Musée de l'Hospice de Villeneuve-lès-Avignon
Photographie Giraudon, Paris VI

Plate III (Page 43)
From manuscript "Les Très Riches Heures du Duc de Berry"
Musée Condé, Chantilly
Etablissements Braun & Cie., Mulhouse

Plate IV (Page 45)
Piet Mondrian: "Composition 1928"
Mart Stam Collection, Amsterdam
From 1959 Art Calender, Verlag Woldemar Klein,
Baden-Baden

Plate V (Page 59)
Francisco Zurbarán: "Lemons, Oranges and Rose"
Coll. A. Contini-Bonacossi, Florence
Photograph by André Held, Ecublens, Lausanne

Plate VI (Page 61)
Rembrandt: "Man in Golden Helmet"
Stiftung Staatliche Museen (Gemäldegalerie), Berlin
Etablissements Braun & Cie., Mulhouse

Plate VII (Page 63)
Pablo Picasso: "Guitar on Mantelpiece"
Privately owned
Etablissements Braun & Cie., Mulhouse
© 1973, Copyright by SPADEM, Paris, and COSMO-PRESS, Geneva

Plate VIII (Page 69)
"La Belle Verrière", Chartres
Photographie Giraudon, Paris

Plate IX (Page 71)
Mathias Grünewald: "Isenheim altarpiece"
detail
Musée d'Unterlinden, Colmar
Etablissements Braun & Cie., Mulhouse

Plate X (Page 73)
Auguste Renoir: "Le Moulin de la Galette"
detail
Musée National du Louvre (Jeu de Paume et Orangerie), Paris
Etablissements Braun & Cie., Mulhouse
© 1973, Copyright by SPADEM, Paris, and COSMO-Press, Geneva

Plate XI (Page 74)
Claude Monet: "Houses of Parliament in Fog"
Musée National du Louvre (Jeu de Paume et Orangerie), Paris
SCALA, Istituto Fotografico Editoriale, Antella (Firenze)
© 1973, Copyright by SPADEM, Paris, and COSMO-PRESS, Geneva

Plate XII (Page 77)
Paul Cézanne: "Apples and Oranges"
Musée National du Louvre (Jeu de Paume et Orangerie), Paris
Etablissements Braun & Cie., Mulhouse

Plate XIII (Page 81)
Jan van Eyck: "Madonna of the Chancellor Rolin"
Musée National du Louvre, Paris
Etablissements Braun & Cie., Mulhouse

Plate XIV (Page 83)
Piero della Francesca: "Solomon Receiving the Queen of Sheba"
San Francesco, Arezzo
SCALA, Istituto Fotografico Editoriale, Antella (Firenze)
Paul Cézanne: "Mont Sainte-Victoire"

Plate XV (Page 85)
Museum of Art, Philadelphia
Etablissements Braun & Cie., Mulhouse

Plate XVI (Page 91)
From manuscript "Apocalypse de Saint Sever"
Service Photographique,
Bibliothèque Nationale, Paris

Plate XVII (Page 93)
El Greco: "Stripping of Christ"
Alte Pinakothek, Munich
Photograph by Blauel, Munich

Plate XVIII (Page 95)
Vincent van Gogh: "Café at Evening"
Rijksmuseum Kröller-Müller, Otterloo
Etablissements Braun & Cie., Mulhouse